Managing the Primary School Budget

An Introduction for Teachers and Governors

Brent Davies & Linda Ellison

Northcote House

British Library Cataloguing in Publication Data
Davies, Brent
Managing the primary school budget: an introduction for teachers
  and governors. (Resources in education).
  1. Great Britain. Primary schools. Financial management
  I. Title II. Ellison, Linda III. Series
  372 12060941

ISBN 0-7463-0592-3

First published in 1990 by Northcote House Publishers Ltd,
Plymbridge House, Estover Road, Plymouth PL6 7PZ, United
Kingdom. Tel: (0752) 705251. Fax: (0752) 777603. Telex: 45635.

Typeset by PDQ Typesetting, Stoke-on-Trent
Printed in Great Britain by BPCC Wheatons Ltd, Exeter

Managing the Primary School Budget

An Introduction for Teachers and Governors

North Lanarkshire Council
Education Resource Service,
8, Kildonan Street,
Coatbridge, ML5 3LP
Telephone (01236) 434377

Resources in Education

Other titles in this Series:

Contents

Acknowledgements

Brian Cox, LMS Manager, Cheshire County Council, for advice about the content of the book.

Hazel Davies, for help in producing the book.

Peter Levell, Deputy County Education Officer, Surrey, for advice and permission to include the material in Appendix One.

Isabel Smith, Head of East Street First School, Leek, Staffordshire, for help and advice on all aspects of the book.

Ken Wild, Head of LMS Training, Surrey, for his time, enthusiasm and management knowledge in developing the material for this book.

Preface

A great deal has been written about Local Management of Schools (LMS) and its introduction into the education system. However, most of the books and articles focus on the developments at the Local Education Authority level especially concerning the development of the formula for funding schools. What is now needed is material that will help the primary sector implement good LMS practice at the school level. This book aims to fill the gap in the LMS literature and provide practical step by step advice for primary schools to help them operate in this new framework of LMS.

It is the fundamental belief of the authors of this book that primary schools exist to provide effective education in a secure and caring environment. Schools are not merely budgetary centres; staff, heads and governors should not be obsessed with administration and finance to the detriment of the basic educational mission. However, if schools are to be effective educational institutions in the 1990s, those involved in management will need the skills to operate the new responsibilities in the resource management field. This book develops those skills and demonstrates how finance can be managed to facilitate the education process in schools.

The book is arranged in three main sections with a summary of the key management implications at the end. Section A sets the framework of LMS and looks at the income and expenditure elements of a primary school budget. It is divided into three chapters: in Chapter 1 the basic structure of the LMS funding process from LEAs to schools is outlined, and there is a discussion of the impact of the change on primary schools. Chapter 2 gives a step by step analysis of the way in which a school receives its income by means of the LEA formula. This allows the reader to check how his/her school compares with the outline process. Chapter 3 looks at the key aspects of expenditure in the budget.

Having established the financial framework of LMS the book moves on, in Section B, to consider two key aspects of managing

LMS: Chapter 4 establishes the position of budgetary management within the framework of the whole School Development Plan; Chapter 5 reviews the role of the partners in the school, the staff, head and governors, in managing LMS. It is only by considering the people and the wider school context that finance can be effectively managed. This having been achieved, the book then moves on to practical school-based budgeting.

Section C consists of four chapters which concentrate on the way in which the budgetary process works in a typical primary school: Chapter 6 outlines a case study school giving background information, a curriculum review, a staffing review, a premises review and Form 7 and budgetary information. With this basic information the following three chapters set out the practical steps of *budgetary review* (Chapter 7), *budgetary forecasting* (Chapter 8), and *budgetary implementation* (Chapter 9) to show how a typical school would manage its budget.

The book ends by reviewing the key implications for primary school managers in the new LMS framework.

This guide aims, therefore, to provide those involved with primary school management with the basic practical help they now need to cope with their new-found responsibilities.

1

The Nature and Dimensions of LMS

This chapter aims to establish a broad understanding of the significance and structure of LMS. It will do so by reviewing

- the nature of the change that LMS is bringing to the education system
- the way in which finance is distributed from the LEA to the school, and
- the impact on primary school management of the reforms encompassed in the Education Reform Act (1988).

THE NATURE OF THE CHANGE

Local Management of Schools (LMS) centres on transferring a considerable area of responsibility from the Local Education Authority (LEA) to the school. While it does transfer much financial autonomy to schools it is a mistake to consider LMS simply as decentralising financial decision-making. It changes the whole nature of the management of primary schools and therefore calls for significant changes in the role of headteachers, governors and school staff in order to meet the challenge of this reform.

The majority of teachers feel that the National Curriculum is by far the most significant component of the 1988 Education Reform Act (ERA). It is the one which seems to have the most direct effect on the children. In some LEAs there is also a growing awareness that Open Enrolment, Grant Maintained Schools and City Technology Colleges are having an impact because they are creating a competitive environment. LMS, however, is viewed by many teachers as the component of ERA which is furthest removed from the pupils and, indeed, from the staff themselves. When it comes to managing the budget they believe that this is something which the governors and the head will deal with and that they themselves have no role to play.

This is taking a very superficial view of LMS, because its implications have the potential to reshape the education service in ways which go far beyond any other aspect of the Act. The changes will be seen at the level of the whole system, the LEA, the individual school, the teacher and the pupil.

There is a tendency to concentrate on the delegation of funds and of responsibility for them, but the major feature of LMS is the *devolution of power* to the school level. The opportunity to make major budgetary decisions is just one manifestation of this power. Much has been written about Local Financial Management (LFM) pilot schemes which operated up to April 1990 but, although there are lessons to be learned from these, they were not formula-based and governors did not have the delegated staffing powers which LEAs are phasing in by April 1993. These 'new' features make LMS significantly different in kind from LFM.

A common misconception is that LMS will *necessitate* primary school heads spending large amounts of their time working on matters associated with the budget. There is a danger that heads will concentrate on administrative solutions to managerial problems. They may spend hours making contact with decorators, glaziers etc, writing orders and poring over balance sheets – all operations which could be done by a secretary. Heads would soon lose much of their present contact with the pupils and the staff. This may be true in the early stages but it is not a desirable development. Heads should be performing more strategic functions such as forecasting and forward planning. This should be done in consultation with staff who can then help to generate alternative courses of action which will inform budgetary decisions.

The first process to be understood by the partners in the school is the way in which finance is distributed from the LEA to the school. This will be examined in the next section.

THE OVERALL FRAMEWORK OF LEA FINANCE

The overall allocation of resources from LEAs to schools can be shown by the following diagram. Each of the stages in the sequence will be taken in turn to explain how finance is distributed to schools.

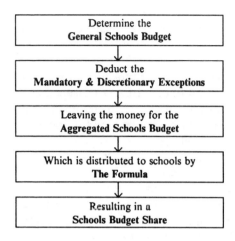

General Schools Budget
This is the total amount of money allocated by an LEA during a
financial year, either to be spent directly on primary, middle and
secondary schools, or on costs attributable to them. Thus it includes
not only money spent at the school level but all central LEA expenses
incurred in administering and managing the education service for
these schools. The total amount of money for the General Schools
Budget (GSB) is determined by the Local Authority when it receives
its funding from the business rate, community charge and central
government grant. From this GSB will be deducted funds for
mandatory and discretionary exceptions before the amount that is
distributed to schools is determined.

Mandatory Exceptions
LEAs are obliged under the 1988 Act to keep central control over
certain areas of expenditure called mandatory exceptions. These areas
are:

1. Capital expenditure
2. Debt charges
3. Specific Grants:
   (a) Education Support Grants
   (b) LEA Training Grants
   (c) Section 11 Grants (for children whose first language is not
       English)

(d) Travellers' Children Grants
(e) TVEI (Technical and Vocational Educational Initiative)
4. EEC grants

When these specific grants are provided through central government there is a requirement (on the LEA) to ensure that they are spent for their intended purpose. They are, therefore, allocated to qualifying schools and the money cannot be used for any other purpose, either at LEA or school level.

Discretionary Exceptions
These are areas of expenditure over which authorities may choose to retain central control or which may be delegated to schools by the formula (see page 13). Discretionary exceptions are divided into two groups: open-ended discretionary exceptions, and those which must not exceed 10% (later to be 7%) of the GSB.

1. *Open-ended discretionary exceptions*
These may (and in most LEAs do) include:

- central administration
- inspectors/advisers
- home to school transport
- school meals
- premature retirement costs and severance pay
- governors' insurance
- transitional exceptions – normally grounds & cleaning contracts, where these had started before April 1990

2. *Discretionary exceptions subject to 10% limit*
Most, but not all, LEAs include in this category:

- structural maintenance
- premises insurance
- statemented pupils
- educational psychologists and educational welfare officers
- school library & museum services
- peripatetic teachers
- funds to permit LEA initiatives
- special staff costs (cover for magistrates and union duties, long-term sickness and maternity leave)
- contingencies

There is also scope to include other approved items such as resource centres and outdoor centres.

While these costs must not, at the outset, exceed 10% GSB, there is a requirement to reduce this figure to 7% by 1994. Many LEAs have started with a figure of 8 or 9% and so are now looking to delegate some of these items. Those authorities which have started at below 7% tend to have devolved funds for peripatetic teachers and library and museum services so that schools now choose whether to buy from the traditional supplier, or from elsewhere, or to spend the money on other areas.

Aggregated Schools Budget (ASB)
This is the sum of money which remains for allocation to schools once funding for mandatory and discretionary exceptions has been set aside.

The Formula
The formula is applied to the ASB in order to determine the School Budget Share (see below) for each school. The formula used by an LEA must meet the criteria laid down by the DES and must have been approved by the DES.
For example, it must:

- be simple, clear and predictable in its impact;
- be based on an assessment of need, rather than on historic expenditure patterns;
- distribute at least 75% of the ASB according to pupil numbers, which may be weighted according to age;
- fund schools on average (rather than actual) teacher costs.

The formula varies from one LEA to another, but typically the age-weighted pupil unit (AWPU) part (at least 75%) is based on staffing (teaching and non-teaching) and capitation costs in an average school, according to LEA policies. The 'other factors' part (up to 25%) is based on allowances for rates, internal repairs, energy, special deprivation and so on, and should include allowances for curriculum protection in small schools and for supporting Special Educational Needs.

The School Budget Share
When the Aggregated Schools Budget is distributed to schools by the formula the result will be a sum of money, called the School Budget Share, for each school. This sum of money will be to cover for example:

- staffing – teaching and non-teaching
- capitation – books and educational materials
- office expenses & telephones
- premises – energy, rates, water rates
- non-structural repairs and maintenance
- furniture and equipment
- insurance
- contingencies including pay and price increases

The budget share is cash-limited (ie an allowance for inflation is built into it). The school has to manage within it unless there are exceptional circumstances such as large, unforeseen rises in pupil roll.

Delegation of the School Budget Share
By April 1993 (1994 in the ex-ILEA authorities) power to control the budget share *must* be given to the governors of the following:

- all secondary/high schools
- all 9-13 middle schools
- all 8-12 middle schools with 200 or more pupils
- all primary schools with 200 or more pupils

In the period leading up to this date the situation will vary between, and even within, individual LEAs. Most are operating some form of phased introduction, either to an ever-growing number of schools or of a widening range of spending categories.

There is no legal requirement to devolve budgetary power to primary (or 8-12 middle) schools with fewer than 200 pupils. However, for various reasons, many authorities are including them in schemes, although sometimes using a longer implementation timescale.

Whether or not governors have delegated powers, all schools must exist on their budget shares from April 1990. There is, however, the opportunity for 'cushioning' (a term used to mean limited protection): a school would be funded according to the formula but would have this budget adjusted over a four-year period if the amount differed from its historic budget. The schools that 'lose' money would typically have to bear only 20% of that loss in the first year of the LEA scheme, 40% the second year, and so on. The gainers would only be allowed to keep 20% of the gain the first year, 40% the second year and so on until they reach 100% (see page 27). In some LEAs different figures are used and often this cushioning is applied only to the staffing element. Also there is the possibility of an LEA opting to extend cushioning to protect the 'big losers'.

The way in which a typical LEA organises its distribution mechanism is illustrated in the Appendix where Peter Levell, Deputy County Education Officer, explains how Surrey established its LMS scheme.

Having considered how the broader aspects of LMS function between LEAs and schools, the focus moves in the final section of this chapter to consider what these and other changes will mean for primary schools in the 1990s.

IMPLICATIONS FOR PRIMARY SCHOOL MANAGEMENT

The implications for primary school management can best be understood by examining five interlinked concepts which emerge from the Education Reform Act and turn LMS into a significant part of a wider revolution in school management. These concepts are:

- formula funding
- delegated finance
- staffing delegation
- open enrolment
- performance indicators

Formula Funding
Because it directly relates the amount of finance to the number of children, formula funding makes a school accountable in a 'market' sense to the parents who send their children there. If the school is perceived as being successful then parents will keep their children there and new children will be attracted. Conversely, if it is perceived as being unsuccessful, parents may remove their children and new entrants will not be attracted. Consequently as children move in or out of the school the level of funding will rise or fall. Successful schools will be rewarded and unsuccessful ones will be put under financial pressure. Thus it becomes vital for schools not only to

provide quality education but to be perceived by their clients to be doing so. This means that attention must be paid to marketing and managing the school's reputation.

Delegated Finance

Delegated finance has two key factors for schools to consider. Firstly, the school will not receive an individual budget for staffing, energy, equipment and so on. Instead it receives a lump sum which it then divides. This means that the school will have to set its own spending priorities and allocate the money between the expenditure categories as it sees fit. It is important that schools should not automatically follow the previous expenditure patterns (an incremental approach) but rather take a fresh look at whether levels of spending in different categories can be justified (a zero based approach). This element of choice in expenditure is one which is new to schools; it requires new skills on the part of those in school management so that they can relate resource choices and educational needs.

Secondly, the school will be able to move money from one expenditure area to another during the financial year, a process known as **virement**. Unlike previous practice (where money, once allocated, was lost if not totally spent), savings can now be effectively utilised within the school. This means the school not only sets initial priorities but can adjust spending patterns to meet changed circumstances as the financial year progresses.

Staffing Delegation

Staffing delegation to the school under LMS has two important aspects. Firstly, levels of staffing will fluctuate with the level of finance, which in turn is determined by the changing numbers of children. This, in itself, should give each member of staff a real incentive to provide a quality service for the clients. However, for those managing the school, the nature and permanence of employees' contracts may need to be reviewed to ensure some flexibility so that staffing levels can reflect changing resource levels.

Secondly, at the school, the governors, in consultation with the head, will be responsible for appointing, disciplining and dismissing staff. In the case of dismissal, the governors decide that a member of staff is 'no longer required at the school' and the LEA then actually issues the redundancy letter. Therefore new skills in personnel management will have to be learned to manage this complex responsibility effectively.

Open Enrolment
This allows parents to choose the school which their child attends or to move them from the existing school to a new one, subject to places being available. Traditional school catchment areas will not, in the early 1990s, be the determinants of a school's roll. While many children will obviously come from the immediate area, a growing number of parents will be free to move their children to the school of their choice. It is important for schools to realise that parents make choices on both rational and other grounds. A school may think that its language development policy and its maths scheme are the key factors that parents perceive as being important, but this may not always be the case. Schools may be chosen because of the approachability of the head and staff, or because of all kinds of idiosyncratic factors. With open enrolments it is important to consider not just the obvious perceptions about the school, but a host of other factors.

Performance Indicators
These can best be thought of as overt or covert. Overt performance indicators are the ones with which educationalists will be familiar. A good example would be scores of reading and mathematical ability. While these indicators may be very significant in parents' minds when they judge the performance of the school, they may not be the only ones. When the parents wait for the five year old child at the school gate, the two dominant factors may well be whether or not he or she wears a school sweatshirt and brings home a reading book. This is because wearing a school sweatshirt is associated in the parents' minds with a school uniform which, in turn, equates with school discipline. Bringing the reading book home is perceived as 'homework' and a sign of academic standards. Both of these factors are covert performance indicators but, nonetheless, are very important for parents. When considering how the community evaluates a school, school management should be aware that it is being done on these two different levels. Choice of school may be determined by either of the performance indicator categories and the level of funding will adjust accordingly. It is important to realise that it is not sufficient to be a good school – one must be perceived as being good as well.

THE IMPORTANCE OF RESOURCE MANAGEMENT

While these five factors are very significant in analysing the impact of LMS on school management, the overriding factor is how resources are used in school development planning. Only schools which have clear educational goals, objectives and plans to achieve them can hope to manage resources effectively from an educational point of view. Therefore the importance of school development planning and the place of budgeting within it is crucial, an issue which will be considered in Chapter 4.

This chapter has outlined the broad principles of LMS. Chapter 2 provides a framework that a primary school can use when assessing the income part of its budget. Chapter 3 will then consider the costs and expenditure side of the budget.

2
The Primary School Budget: Income

This chapter reviews the way in which primary schools generate their income within the new LMS framework. The chapter is arranged in six main sections:

- Income related to Pupil Roll and Age Weighting
- Premises-related income
- Targeted income factors
- Income from transitional funding
- Other LEA income
- Non-LEA income

The following explanation of each of these sections should enable readers to check their experience against the outline provided.

1. INCOME RELATED TO PUPIL ROLL AND AGE WEIGHTING

As explained more fully below, this involves working out the pupil roll for the school, adjusting it for any age weighting and multiplying the result by the relevant unit of resource. The unit of resource is a sum of money (eg £850) allocated for each unit of weighting. For example, if a child is weighted 1 and the unit of resource is £850 the school will receive £850 for that child.

Calculating the Pupil Roll
LEAs have adopted some significant variations in how they calculate the pupil roll for the financial year. Heads and governors should be aware of these – and of the implications for their schools. The most common methods used are:

(a) the numbers on roll in the January preceding the financial year. These numbers are determined by reference to the Department of Education (DES) Form 7. This system favours schools with a static or falling roll as finance will be based on numbers which are lagging behind current lower numbers;

(b) a proportion of the number on roll (according to Form 7) in the January preceding the financial year and a proportion based on the estimated figures for the following January's Form 7. The proportions are 5/12ths January actuals + 7/12ths next January's projections. This system works in favour of schools whose roll will increase; it is therefore particularly beneficial to primary schools with a two or three intake pattern. Sometimes there are specific adjustments for Easter intakes as well.

It will be possible, when the LEA formulae are reviewed in future years, to make representations to alter the basis of the calculation. The nature of these representations may be coloured according to whether a school has a rising or declining roll!

With both these methods of calculation it is very important for schools to ensure that correct figures are used. Previously, incorrect recording meant losing £20 to £30 of capitation per child but now it means losing a complete unit of resource which (at 1990 figures) is about £800 to £900 in a primary school. LEAs retain a contingency fund which may be used to compensate schools whose rolls fluctuate significantly from the original position ('significant' is defined as anywhere between 3% and 10% or a fixed number). However, most LEAs are only giving additional funding for the number of children *above* the threshold.

Age Weighting

The pupil numbers are then multiplied by an age weighting in order to establish the total 'age-weighted pupil units' (usually abbreviated as AWPU). There may be marginal enhancement for certain age groups in the primary school (usually the lower and upper end) so it is worth checking that pupils have been carefully recorded in the correct age band.

When the value of an AWPU for the financial year is known, this is multiplied by the school's total AWPU and a cash sum is generated for the school (see pages 72-3).

Scope of funding

The funding which derives from the above calculations is intended to cover the cost of staffing, educational materials, office expenditure and so on. The other elements which make up the School Budget Share are based on a variety of factors, although often there is a roll-related element in the calculation.

2. PREMISES-RELATED INCOME

Certain areas of expenditure are not directly related to the number of pupils in the school although this may have a bearing on the funds needed. The premises-related costs include rent, rates and water rates, repairs and maintenance, energy, cleaning and caretaking, grounds maintenance and, in some LEAs, furniture. To fund these areas of expenditure various calculations are used to determine income in each of the following categories.

Rent and Rates
Because these vary from school to school and cannot be controlled by the school, many LEAs are funding them at actual cost. In some LEAs sewerage charges are including in this category; in others they are calculated separately.

Water Rates and Sewerage Charges
LEAs have various ways of calculating the funding for this:

(a) directly related to pupil roll;
(b) directly related to pupil roll weighted for age;
(c) partly on area of the school and partly according to roll (such as 60% and 40%).

Extra funding is given to schools with swimming pools and there may be some income to compensate for school meals usage.

Repairs and Maintenance
The school will be responsible for the repair and maintenance of certain parts of the school building. This is on a 'landlord and tenant' basis: the LEA agrees to maintain the structural fabric and engineering services while the school maintains what is mainly the internal fabric. The actual responsibilities vary between authorities and should be carefully checked. For example, the school may be responsible for external items such as repairing walls and fences but not for the maintenance of internal equipment such as boilers. There may also be the need to maintain the caretaker's house, although there should be some income partially to offset this expenditure.

Calculations which determine the income to meet repairs and maintenance are based on a variety of factors (that are used in differing combinations) such as:

- floor area
- occupancy rate
- pupil roll
- level of vandalism
- age of building
- condition of building
- type of construction
- weather exposure

This is part of the budget which arouses great controversy, particularly in schools which have been badly maintained by the LEA in previous years. Although some authorities have included a 'condition factor' or have pledged to improve those schools which have fallen behind, there is a strong feeling that new or recently refurbished schools will have a big advantage. Certain authorities, such as Surrey, have agreed to ensure that all schools which have not been decorated in the five years up to 1990 will be decorated at the LEA's expense as soon as is practicable.

Another reason for controversy is the problems anticipated if the LEA fails to maintain the outside of the building so that internal damage results, eg when faults in the roof cause damage to internal decoration. Schools may need to persist in their demands for action in this area. It is important to notify the LEA of any repairs which fall to it in the capacity of 'landlord' so that cases of damage caused by negligence do not arise.

Schools would be wise to take advantage of the services (if available) of the LEA Buildings Inspectors for an annual survey of the internal condition of the school. Otherwise, someone else, either a governor, member of the staff or parent, should monitor the condition and indicate priorities.

Energy

The income under this heading is intended to provide for the cost of heating and lighting the building. Historical information has been quite unreliable as an indicator of need: some schools have been less thrifty, recent winters have been mild and, in many cases, records were not kept for individual schools. Most formulae are based on a combination of floor area, fuel type and pupil numbers. As with the water rates, extra allowances are given to schools which heat a swimming pool (so they should check that this has been included) and there may be income from the school meals service.

Cleaning and Caretaking

Initially the funds that provide for the *cleaning* of schools will, in many LEAs, be a discretionary exception because the LEA is already committed to an existing contract. If the contract has not gone out to tender by the time the school receives a delegated budget then funds for this would be provided in the SBS, usually based on floor area. As existing contracts expire cleaning will no longer be a discretionary exception – the funds will be delegated to the schools. When the school governors have control of this area of expenditure there are two options:

(a) to ask the LEA to make the arrangements for them;
(b) to make their own tendering arrangements, either directly with a
     private contractor or through a school-based organisation.

The school could, at this stage, decide to enhance the specification if it is prepared to pay to have areas cleaned more frequently than the LEA recommendation. There is no need to accept the lowest tender, simply to ensure that value for money is provided.

Whether or not this area of expenditure is delegated to the school, the school has a right to demand that the specification is met by the company.

The income for the *caretaking* part of budget is normally calculated on floor area, perhaps with a flat rate sum as well. For example, in Cheshire there is a fixed sum for any primary school to represent 24 hours duty per week. There is a changed role for the caretaker which usually involves some cleaning (in small schools it will be all the cleaning) and may perhaps involve carrying out minor repairs and maintenance tasks.

Grounds Maintenance

As with school cleaning, the funds for this area of expenditure, where the LEA may be already committed to a contract before the schools receive delegated budgets, may be treated as a discretionary exception. Once funds are delegated, the sum will usually be calculated according to the area of the grounds, possibly with some allowance for the number of pupils or the ratio of grass to hard surfaces.

Furniture
Many authorities have included this in the pupil unit of resource but some have done separate calculations related to the pupil roll, age factors and existing condition.

3. TARGETED INCOME FACTORS

Various other factors are included in the formula to allow LEAs to provide funds according to the needs of individual schools. How these factors are calculated varies considerably from one authority to another so the examples given below are a general guide to current practice.

Flat Rate Allocation
Many LEAs provide a base level of funding according to sector. This is intended to favour smaller schools because it represents a greater proportion of their total income than in larger schools. It is provided either as a cash sum or as an allocation of pupil units which is then converted into a cash sum once the value of a pupil unit for the year is known.

Small School Curriculum Protection
The DES considers that LEAs should take account of the comparatively high cost of operating small schools. The definition of 'small' varies with the age range of the school and from one LEA to another (examples in the primary sector might be 120 for an infant school and 180 for a Junior and Infant school). Typically, a per capita sum would be added (or the AWPU enhanced) to bring the school up to the minimum level considered viable within that sector. Although it is worth checking in a particular LEA, the protection is usually tapered so that a school is not unduly penalised if it recruits one or two extra pupils and thus falls outside the definition of a small school. Individual LEAs may be offering other benefits to small schools such as extra supply cover to facilitate INSET.

Small School Salary Protection
Most LEAs have taken the opportunity to help with salary costs in schools which have a head, and fewer than eleven staff. This applies

where funding the school on average salary costs for the LEA leads to the school having a deficit when compared with higher actual salary costs in that particular school. The DES signals that this provision should be reviewed and that the aim should be gradually to phase it out; some LEAs have stated this intention in their schemes. The DES requires this protection to be scaled to prevent undue penalisation and the protection typically rises from 60% to 100% of the additional salary bill (over and above the sector average).

Surrey for example uses the following scale:

Number of staff including head	Difference between actual and average costs met by the LEA
11.99	60%
10	65%
9	75%
8	85%
7	100%

As another example, Cheshire, which uses the Audit Commission recommended formula, compensates as follows:

Number of teachers including head	% salary bill paid at actual costs	% salary bill paid at sector average costs
12	No protection	No protection
11	20%	80%
10	40%	60%
9	60%	40%
8	80%	20%
up to 7	Actual salaries paid	Actual salaries paid

Split Site
Many LEAs are providing some form of support in order to reflect the burdens which fall on schools with split sites. This is usually a block sum or is related in some way to the pupil roll.

Nursery Units and Pre-five Classes
A lump sum or a per capita enhancement is usually given to allow

schools to provide the necessary assistance, for example to employ a nursery nurse.

Special Educational Needs

The DES expects LEAs to take account of the fact that some 20% of children have special needs at some time in their school life (as well as children who are statemented). LEAs have found it very difficult to quantify this factor and research into more accurate information continues. Many authorities state that part of this provision is included with the AWPU as well as a separate item. The distribution methods used initially include:

(a) a fixed sum for each child claiming free school meals (although it is accepted that such data would not necessarily reflect Special Educational Need). In this situation schools would need to find ways of persuading parents to register and take up their entitlement in order to raise the school's resourcing from this factor;

(b) a sum based on the result of testing at 7 and 11 which reveals the number of children with a low reading score (typically below 70 or 85). However, schools could see this as a disincentive to their work in improving reading skills as they would lose funds by improving children's abilities!

Social Disadvantage

As with the previous factor, measurements of social disadvantage are usually related in some way to parental application for free school meals (as opposed to notional entitlement). Two of the methods of calculating this income are:

(a) the number of pupils claiming x unit of resource;
(b) (percentage claiming)^2 × unit of resource. This is the NFER recommended method.

Both these methods taper the funding to reflect need, and do not involve the use of unfair steps.

 NB. Both with special needs and social disadvantage the method of calculation may only be triggered when the number of pupils qualifying reaches a certain percentage. It is very important to know where the school lies in such a pattern: if it lies close to the threshold at which funding is triggered it could be highly beneficial to find ways of crossing the threshold.

Ethnic Minorities and Forces Families
Some LEAs include a per capita sum (in addition to Section 11 funding) to allow for the extra costs of running a school where there are pupils from recognised ethnic minorities. Similarly, the problems which arise because of the mobility of service families may be recognised in the formula. Both of these funds are, in some schemes, only triggered when a certain percentage is exceeded.

4. INCOME FROM TRANSITIONAL FUNDING

When the size of the Aggregated Schools Budget (ASB) is known and all the above factors are taken into account, it will be possible to calculate the formula-based SBS (see page 73). As indicated in Chapter 1 page 15, this may not, in the early stages of LMS, be the sum which the school receives. In order to cushion the effects of formula funding for the 'losers', most LEAs are operating transitional arrangements whereby the school receives part of its funds based on the formula and part based on what it would have received had the old funding system been continued. There are several variations, the most common of which calculates a percentage of the budget based on the new formula and a percentage based on the historical method as in this example from Leeds:

	1990	1991	1992	1993	1994
Formula	20%	40%	60%	80%	100%
Historic	80%	60%	40%	20%	0%

An alternative approach (which gives the same result) is to calculate the difference between the formula allocation and the allocation had historic funding policies been continued. The school then receives the formula allocation plus or minus a percentage of the difference between the two. For example:

- In the case of a 'gaining' school the budget on a historic funding basis could be £300,000 while on a formula basis it is £320,000. The difference is a gain of £20,000.
- In the case of a 'losing' school with a historic budget of £320,000 and a formula budget of £300,000 the difference is a loss of £20,000.

In the first year (1990) it would work like this:
Winning   £320,000 – 80% of £20,000   Budget = £304,000
School
Losing   £300,000 + 80% of £20,000   Budget = £316,000
School

In the second year (1991) it would work like this:
Winning   £320,000 – 60% of £20,000   Budget = £308,000
School
Losing   £300,000 + 60% of £20,000   Budget = £312,000
School

In the third year (1992) it would work like this:
Winning   £320,000 – 40% of £20,000   Budget = £312,000
School
Losing   £300,000 + 40% of £20,000   Budget = £308,000
School

In 1993 the final phase of adjustment of 20% would take place and in 1994 the schools would be operating full formula budgets.

Further implications of cushioning
Such cushioning operates against the 'winners' because, in many LEAs, they do not receive their full entitlement under LMS until 1994. For losers there is the problem of managing on a constantly reducing budget while retaining staff morale and motivation. It has been suggested that fairly drastic 'cuts' should be made quite early on so that there is not a cloud hanging over the staff for four years. However this may be a mistake as it is important to take a longer term view of the budget and plan the effect of any changes over a number of years in order to set adjustments in context. Whatever the approach, careful long term planning will help staff to know what to expect so that they do not feel unduly threatened.

Having calculated the sum to be received during the year, it is important to realise that it is cash-limited, ie that it includes provision for pay and price increases and for contingencies. Only in very exceptional circumstances (which are clearly laid down in each scheme) can a school turn to the LEA for additional help.

5. OTHER LEA INCOME

As well as income generated by the standard LEA formula, various other LEA sums of money come into a school. They take the form of compensation for expenses not incurred during normal school use but which the school has to bear.

Caretaker's house
If a school has a caretaker's house, the same landlord and tenant relationship with the LEA will apply as for the main school buildings. The statement of income will probably show some form of rental income or LEA subsidy to enable the school to meet the extra responsibilities.

Directed lettings
If the LEA specifies that the school *must* be let for certain adult education or community use activities then the school receives the standard LEA rate for these activities, eg a fixed hourly rate for use of the hall, rooms or grounds. Schools may find, through careful monitoring, that this is not an economical rate and that such activities are a drain on the school's budget. If this is so, the governors should ask the LEA to change the rate or, perhaps, to stop using that school. A particular problem would arise if only one group is using one room for one hour but the whole school is having to be heated. An investment in zonal heating controls could be very valuable for the school!

Payments in respect of the School Meals Service
This is in recognition of the fact that (unless there is separate metering) the school is paying water rates and energy costs incurred during the preparation and serving of meals. The actual compensation system varies considerably between LEAs but, as with directed lettings, governors should press for a revised system if it appears to prejudice the main educational activities. For the supervision of school meals, there is often an income shown for adult meals in order to compensate the school for the cost of providing meals for lunchtime supervisors. Any free lunches which staff take in addition to this will fall as a cost to the school.

6. NON-LEA INCOME

There are a number of methods open to the school to raise extra income. When faced with a shortfall of funds a school should not immediately consider cutting expenditure but should look at other possible methods of generating income. It is important to consider the effort needed to raise such funds. If it takes a school a whole term to raise £1,000 it has to be borne in mind that this is only slightly more than the income from one extra child and perhaps energies would be better directed towards marketing and recruitment. Some possible areas for consideration are outlined below.

Lettings
The school is free to decide the charge for lettings (except for those directed by the LEA) but needs to bear in mind a number of points. For example what will be the extra costs of lettings such as cleaning, caretaking, energy, wear and tear, potential damage and the responsibility for insurance? Income must of course cover these expenses unless there are significant other reasons. The way of calculating the charge and deciding whether or not profit should always be the motive needs a clear management policy and clear lines of responsibility as to who makes the decisions.

Charges
Charges may be made for services which the school is able to offer such as photocopying, loan of equipment, the siting of advertising boards, etc.

Sponsorship
This can bring funds, materials, equipment or expertise into the school. But will the companies or products be acceptable to the staff and parents, and how far should the core areas of school activity be supported in this way?

Covenants and other donations
The former provide regular income while the latter may only be occasional. The opportunities in this area depend very much upon the socio-economic environment and on the tradition of the school.

PTA

Funds raised by the PTA are usually targeted at specific projects. Although they require a lot of effort, the benefits are wider than just income, extending to promoting the image of the school and providing activities in the local community. Managers need to consider whether or not the use of school premises for such activities as bingo in winter are actually a drain on the school's resources rather than fund raisers.

School fund

Although useful for minor purchases, this area is unlikely to fund major items unless money has been paid in from other income-generating activities.

SUMMARY

This whole area is closely related to marketing and with how the school manages its communications and relationships with the local community. An effective marketing policy which also enhances this process will increase the potential for raising income.

This chapter has examined how schools have obtained money to fund their educational expenditure. The following chapter will discuss the nature of school costs and the pattern of expenditure.

3
The Primary School Budget: Costs and Expenditure

The previous chapter considered the sources of income for a primary school. This chapter considers the nature of the costs that a school faces and goes on to examine the individual items of expenditure.

THE NATURE OF COSTS IN PRIMARY SCHOOLS

In the previous two chapters the significance of pupil numbers has been emphasised because, as these rise or fall, so does the level of funding. Primary schools will have to adjust their spending to accommodate these changes in the level of income if they are to balance their budgets. The ability to adjust levels of expenditure depends on the nature of the underlying costs which trigger that expenditure. One of the useful distinctions which can be drawn is that between fixed and variable costs.

Fixed and Variable Costs

- **Fixed costs** are those which cannot be adjusted quickly as numbers change. Thus, if a Group 4 (new Group 2) primary school of 230 pupils had a fall in its roll of 30 pupils (with consequent loss of income), some costs would not change. Typical examples of these would be basic repairs and maintenance, telephone rentals and headteacher's salary.

- **Variable costs** are those which change with the number of pupils in the school. Two good examples of this are class teachers and exercise books. If schools provide one teacher for every 30 children then, as numbers increase, more teachers are taken on and when numbers of children fall, the number of teachers will be reduced. Similarly, the number of exercise books purchased will relate directly to the number of pupils. While the number of exercise books used will increase or reduce with each child, staffing tends to adjust through a series of thresholds, with a number of children needed to trigger a change in levels.

The following represents the continuum of fixed and variable costs in education:

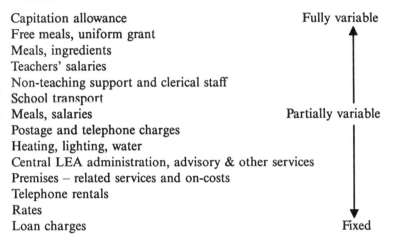

Capitation allowance	Fully variable
Free meals, uniform grant	
Meals, ingredients	
Teachers' salaries	
Non-teaching support and clerical staff	
School transport	
Meals, salaries	Partially variable
Postage and telephone charges	
Heating, lighting, water	
Central LEA administration, advisory & other services	
Premises – related services and on-costs	
Telephone rentals	
Rates	
Loan charges	Fixed

Fixed and variable costs in Education

The significance of these costs can be represented by the diagram, shown overleaf, from Davies & Braund (1989).

A school at point A will be spending 70% of its budget on variable costs such as teachers, books and equipment, and 30% of its budget on fixed costs, mainly premises. If it gains pupils the money they bring in will not have to be spent on fixed costs (the buildings are already maintained) and most of it can be spent on teachers, books and equipment. So at point C although it spends the same amount on its fixed costs they are now a smaller proportion of total costs.

The reverse is true when a school loses pupils. Although it gets less money it still has to meet its fixed costs. As a result these fixed costs take up a bigger share of the budget, leaving less to spend on the variable costs of teachers and materials.

Thus, with open enrolments, where parents can choose which school their children attend, the movement of pupils between schools will have a big effect on budgets. Expanding schools will be able to spend much of their income on teachers and materials and so attract

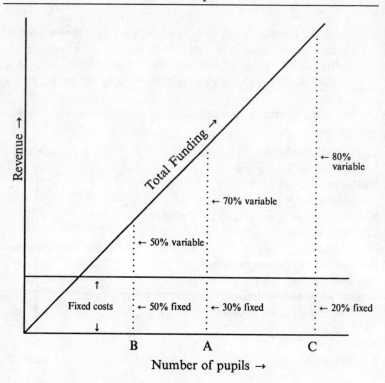

Number of pupils →

even more pupils. The reverse will be true of declining schools. This reinforces the point that LMS is not just a financial change but one that radically alters the nature of the education system.

The significance of fixed and variable costs for the primary school
The primary school faced with changes in its income will have to take a view of which costs it can adjust in the short term.

An increase in pupils will provide funds for an extra teacher but in the short term not an extra classroom; a shortfall in funds due to declining roll may result in the school looking to alternative sources of funds or reducing expenditure. Adjusting staffing levels provides the biggest potential saving but cannot always be done harmoniously, leaving a well-motivated staff or a balanced curriculum. Schools do need to plan the future trends of both income and expenditure so that short term changes can be seen in the light of the longer term School Development Plan.

Having looked at fixed and variable costs, two other types of cost need to be considered before moving on to a more detailed examination of expenditure; these costs are average and marginal costs.

Average and Marginal Costs

Total average costs (often called unit costs) are calculated by dividing the total of money spent in a school by the number of pupils in that school. Thus, if a school costs £500,000 to run and there are 500 pupils, the average cost (or cost per child) is:

$$\frac{£500,000}{500} = £1,000 \text{ per child}$$

Average costs can also be discovered for individual items of expenditure such as staffing. By adding all the staff salaries and other costs (superannuation and national insurance) and dividing by the number of teachers, schools can work out the average cost of a teacher. This is a significant calculation when compared to the average cost of a teacher in an LEA as a whole.

Marginal costs are those associated with each extra child. These are very significant at certain points. One extra child may cause little extra expenditure in terms of books and materials but a succession of extra pupils will mean that at a certain point an extra child will necessitate splitting groups and employing an extra teacher. At this point the extra cost of the marginal child is considerable. Expanding intake is financially viable as long as marginal costs are less than the revenue they bring in. The critical point occurs when a threshold is crossed and the marginal child causes extra staffing or building costs to be incurred.

AREAS OF SCHOOL COSTS AND EXPENDITURE

Staffing Costs

A number of significant management issues arise in assessing staff costs. The first concerns how far these costs are fixed and how far they are variable. Headteachers are a fixed cost as they are on permanent appointments and every school must have one. As pupil numbers increase, the headteacher's salary would marginally increase if the school went up a group size but would not decrease if numbers reduced. However, teachers represent a variable cost because the number employed would fluctuate with the number of pupils.

A second issue arises with assessing the salary costs in a particular year. The financial year starts in April, but very often staffing changes take place at the beginning of the academic year in September. As a result increasing or decreasing staffing levels will not have an effect on the first 5/12ths of the financial year. Careful planning is needed to assess the sequence of academic changes and the time of their financial impact. Similarly, teachers' salaries do not necessarily remain at the level of the 1st April: many have incremental increases in September and recent history suggests that pay awards are often phased over a year so that assessing actual salary costs in one financial year can be a complex problem.

Similar considerations apply to the staffing costs of the non-teaching staff such as:

- Administrative and secretarial staff
- Nursery Assistants and Classroom Assistants
- Caretaking staff
- Midday Supervisors

Virement of staffing costs

The third issue is that of moving money from one area of expenditure to another (virement). While virement can occur across the range of expenditure headings, moving money from the area of staffing to another area offers the largest financial opportunity and also causes the greatest concern to existing staff. However, the flexibility in staffing opportunities which this presents is one that schools should examine. In a school with a headteacher, 10 full time staff and two 0.5 part time staff (where the school is organised into 10 classes with the half time teachers providing support) careful choices would have to be made if one of those part time teachers left. Does the school appoint two half time classroom assistants instead of the one half time teacher—the costs are about the same—or does the school use the money for books and equipment? These choices are unfamiliar to schools previously dependent on allocations and decisions made by the LEA.

Supply cover for absent teachers

The final issue of staffing costs in the primary budget is that of supply cover for absent teachers. Most LEAs will be retaining part of the supply budget (often 25%) to cover long term illness, the remainder being delegated to schools as part of the formula based budget. A school will have to allocate a sum of money from its total budget from which it can 'buy' supply teachers to cover absent staff, usually at the rate of £80 per day. A further option is to take out a commercial insurance policy. If a school decides to 'cope' with absent staff with the headteacher covering the class then the money would be saved and could be 'vired' to other areas of the budget. In some LEAs where it has been difficult to find supply teachers, primary schools have co-operated and 'pooled' their supply money to appoint a full time teacher who is then shared by the group of schools. This sort of flexibility is one of the benefits that LMS brings.

Premises Costs
A number of areas of expenditure come in this category:

- Building maintenance
- Energy
- Rates
- Ground maintenance
- Other costs: cleaning etc

Building maintenance
Schools will have to plan a 'rolling programme' of building maintenance to ensure costs are spread over a number of years. A good example of this is decorating where schools will have to prioritise areas for decoration and attempt to have one or two classrooms painted each year.

Energy
With energy costs it is important to ensure that the pattern of usage is monitored so that areas for savings can be identified. Efficient thermostatic controls can be very effective in controlling costs. An area for concern arises where the school is let for adult education or community use. The school needs to know that it is receiving the full costs of operating in the evening and that it is receiving an adequate financial return. In the energy field zonal heating controls can be a worthwhile investment as they allow parts of the school to be heated when they are let (such as the hall) without incurring the expense of heating the whole school.

Rates
Rates form an item of expenditure which is usually a fixed amount

when put into budget and subsequently the same amount goes out. There is no room for flexibility or manoeuvre here.

Grounds maintenance

Grounds maintenace is one area of school expenditure that is likely to offer plenty of flexibility in the future. Many schools are still bound by the contracts that the LEA have negotiated on their behalf. When these contracts come up for renewal the school will determine which contractor to employ and how much to spend in this area. This also applies to other costs such as cleaning.

Supplies and Services

Areas of expenditure in this category include:

- Office expenses
- Capitation for books and equipment

Contingency Funds

This is a difficult decision area for school governors and heads. The larger the amount kept aside for contingencies, the less that can be immediately spent on the pupils of the school. Also, if larger amounts of money are unspent in the contingency fund and carried over to the next financial year it may signal to the politicians that funding is more than adequate! Conversely, unforeseen problems or opportunities cannot be met or utilised if funding is not made available. Consequently we would recommend that a small amount of money be kept as a contingency fund, 0.5% or 1% of the budget total. This can be kept as a separate item at the beginning of the financial year; if by January no calls on it have been made then it can be reallocated to other expenditure areas.

VIREMENT

One of the great advantages that LMS gives to schools in controlling their own budgets is the possibility of virement. Previously if a school was allocated money for supply teachers or for energy costs associated with heating the premises and not all the money was spent then the money was retained by the LEA. With LMS the surplus money can be moved to another expenditure area and used within the school. It is important that schools do not wait until the end of the financial year to make these re-allocations. If the school is monitoring its expenditure on a monthly basis, then as the year progresses, adjustments can be made and money vired if under-spendings occur. Similarly, if expenditure exceeds targets, money can be moved from underspent areas or from the contingency fund to meet the deficiency.

INCREMENTAL AND ZERO BASED BUDGETING

The case study (page 57) will examine the three main stages in the budgetary process but two concepts underpin each of these stages. These concepts are Incremental Budgeting and Zero-based Budgeting.

- **Incremental budgeting** is where a school takes last year's figure for expenditure and uses it as a base for this year's allocation, adding on a percentage for inflation.

- **Zero-based budgeting** is where the area of expenditure is subjected to a fundamental review; last year's figure is not used as a base, it has to be fundamentally justified before any funds are allocated.

While in practice most schools will operate an incremental approach, it is worthwhile subjecting one or two areas for a zero-based review each year.

The way in which the income and expenditure functions of budgets fit into a whole school perspective will be examined next in Chapter 4 which considers how the budgetary process integrates with School Development Planning.

4
The Integration of Budgeting into the School Development Plan

The last two chapters described the mechanisms whereby funds are allocated to schools and the goods and services on which such funds are spent at the school level. This chapter has a different focus in that it considers a strategic management area, the School Management Development Plan, and the way in which budgetary processes should link into this.

A central factor of LMS is that finance should not be seen as either the starting point or as a separate activity from the education process; it is simply the facilitator of the education process. If schools are to retain their educational mission, finance should be seen as just part of what the school is trying to achieve and not as predetermining the debate on curriculum and other educational matters.

SCHOOL MANAGEMENT DEVELOPMENT PLANS

If we are to ensure effective education for all our children and not be finance-dominated, governors and staff should work together to prepare and carry out a Management Development Plan for the school. This needs to project the school forward over a three to four year period so that change is anticipated and successfully managed. The School Management Development Plan should encompass all aspects of the school's life, integrating plans for the areas outlined in the following diagram:

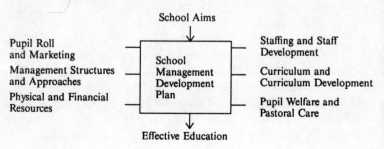

The plan is intended to be a flexible, working document which is responsive to changed circumstances. It involves a continuous cycle of activity so governors and staff will need to consider the stages which are shown and explained below:

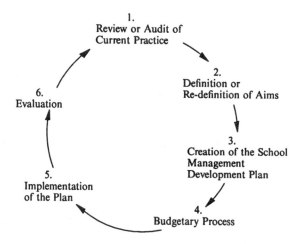

1. Review or audit of current practice

There should be a review or audit of the current position, both within the school and within the wider context of the local community and the education service nationally. The internal review may use informal methods to determine the school's Strengths, Weaknesses, Opportunities and Threats (a SWOT analysis) or more formal evaluation approaches such as GRIDS, or DION (see Glossary). The external review will consider local and national proposals and policies and changes in the local area.

2. Defining school aims

The *aims* of the school are then defined or re-defined to give all partners a clear view and understanding of the school's goals, values and its aspirations for the children in its care.

3. Creating the School Management Development Plan

When these first two activities have been carried out the staff and governors will have to create the **School Management Development Plan**. This will be achieved by translating the general aims into action through laying down specific objectives and making more detailed plans in the following areas:

- management structures and approaches
- curriculum and curriculum development
- staffing and staff development
- pupil welfare and pastoral care
- pupil roll and marketing
- physical resources
- financial resources
- monitoring and evaluation mechanisms

In each of these key areas those involved will have to work through the planning process by generating alternatives, prioritising both in the long and the short term and, later, choosing between alternatives in the decision-making process. The School Management Development Plan will then integrate these detailed plans to give an overall picture of the proposed activities.

4. The budgetary process
The next stage is that of the **budgetary process**. This sets these educational priorities into a financial context and can be seen to comprise four elements:

- a **review** of the existing resource position;

- a **forecasting** or forward planning activity which can set the medium term framework in which the immediate financial decisions are to be made;

- the budgetary **implementation** process during which firm resource decisions are made for the coming financial year;

- an **evaluation** of the way in which resources have been used to meet educational need.

5. Implementing the Plan
This is followed by the **implementation** of the Management Development Plan for the school for the next year. In aspects where change is being implemented schools will have to consider how the change process is to be managed as well as the nature of the change.

6. Evaluation
Finally, there needs to be some form of **evaluation** in order to assess

whether the plans, once implemented, have really achieved the objectives set. The nature of the evaluation should be clarified at the planning stage and several questions must be posed. For example, who will carry out the evaluation? What process will be used? What criteria or performance indicators will be used? Who is the intended audience for the final report?

Having worked through the management cycle, the information from the evaluation stage can be used to inform the next review or audit as the cycle continues again. Aims will be checked for their continued relevance and the details of the School Management Development Plan will be adjusted as necessary.

The budgetary process, the focus of this book, will now be examined in more detail. It will be applied to a practical situation in the case study (Chapters 6 to 9).

THE BUDGETARY PROCESS

Before the process starts, it is necessary to clarify the principles and procedures to be followed in a particular school. The main issue which needs to be considered is how far the partners in the educational process are to be involved in the budgetary process. The roles and responsibilities of these partners (such as governors, staff and parents) need to be clear from the outset. The extent to which they are to be consulted or to take part in the decision-making process needs to be fully understood by those who may feel involved. Problems can soon arise if people think that they are being asked to make decisions when they are, in fact, only being canvassed for their opinions. Chapter 5 considers this area of roles and responsibilities in more detail.

As with the overall Management Development Plan, the budgetary process is a continuous cycle of activity and comprises the same key stages. These are shown below and are then explained briefly. More detailed explanations are to be found in the case study chapters.

1. Budgetary Review

4. Budgetary Evaluation

2. Budgetary Forecasting

3. Budgetary Implementation

1. Budgetary Review

This review should consider the way in which the school has used its resources during the previous year. It needs to be carried out annually although there may be a more detailed analysis of certain areas on a rotating basis. Those planning the review should consider how it is to be structured, who is to gather the information and when the information is to be presented for collation. It would then usually fall to the senior management team to draw the information together and to prioritise the findings so as to inform the next stage of the budgetary process.

Although there will be inevitable overlap, it may be helpful to consider the review in five sections as follows:

- curriculum
- staffing
- physical resources
- support services
- external resources

It would be more efficient and effective (as well as helping staff development) to delegate the work to individuals or teams so as to spread the load and involve all staff. The information will be drawn from monitoring statements and from both formal and informal evaluation procedures. Those preparing the reviews should highlight the key issues rather than submit all their source documents. There should be some evidence of how far resources have been used efficiently and effectively. The timescale for gathering the information needs to be decided according to the school situation. Each aspect of the review will now be considered.

Curriculum

The necessary information should already be available as a result of compiling the 'Curriculum and Curriculum Development' section of the School Management Development Plan. As well as highlighting needs, areas which are adequately supported should be mentioned in order to have an overview of the position. For each area of the curriculum (and for extra-curricular and 'pastoral' areas as appropriate) there should be a statement of resources needed in order to continue to develop the area. Items to be mentioned might include consumables, books, equipment and storage. There would be an overlap with the staffing review here because staffing levels and staff development needs would be highlighted while reviewing the curriculum. Some schools may want the reviews to include a detailed statement of expenditure level in each curricular area.

Staffing
The detail will come from the information which is gathered to inform the 'Staffing and Staff Development' section of the School Management Development Plan. It should include:

- teaching staff profiles – curricular expertise and responsibilities, qualifications and experience, the use made of this expertise
- administrative staff
- classroom support staff
- caretaker
- midday assistants
- recruitment and retention policy and process
- management structure – responsibilities, participation, delegation.

Physical Resources
This review would highlight the condition of the premises and the availability of space in which to carry out the educational and support activities associated with the school. It would consider the utilisation of classrooms, sports facilities, resource areas and other space, including office and staff accommodation, facilities for the caretaker, for storage and for school meals. Access for parents and for the disabled should also be examined.

Some comment about running costs such as energy costs and telephone usage may be relevant.

Support Services
Although there may be overlap between this and other areas in the review, it may be worth highlighting the use of resources for classroom support and office services. This would probably involve the collation of teaching and non-teaching staff opinion.

External Resources
The availability of help from outside the school may affect budgetary decisions. For example, local industry may be prepared to finance the production of the school brochure. If, on the other hand, the LEA is charging for the use of the School Library Service, then that may

have implications for the investment needed in new books at the school level.

This review area would summarise the present level of provision in the natural environment and from individuals and organisations such as:

- LEA and local government services
- parents and PTA
- medical, psychological and social services
- police
- industry and commerce
- secondary schools
- further and higher education institutions
- playgroups and other community groups

When all the individual reviews have been received, someone needs to collate them and to produce a summary document which highlights the resource priorities for the coming financial year. As mentioned earlier, in a primary school this task is likely to fall to the head, deputy or small senior management team. This should be more effective than if the task were left entirely to governors because those who work in the school each day ought to be better able to analyse the needs of the school. The summary document should be quite concise and clear in its recommendation of priorities. However, there should not be an attempt at this stage to 'prune' the list so that it is realistic. It needs to be longer than the school would expect to be able to fund, so that creativity is not stifled.

2. Budgetary Forecasting

Senior managers and governors have to view immediate financial decisions within a longer time frame. Making a financial decision for the current financial year, if it is to be effective, has to be seen in the context of the financial circumstances of the school over the next three or four years. For example, a school with a budget deficit of £2,000 may view it less seriously if its roll is increasing over the succeeding years and hence the level of funding will easily offset that deficit. It will be necessary to make forecasts about the following:

- pupil roll and age profile
- any changes to floor area
- any changes to other factors such as the small school allowance, special needs

- any changes to LEA discretionary exceptions
- any changes to Local Government Act (LGA) contract arrangements
- any other changes to income such as lettings, covenants or sponsorship

This information will allow the school to see a probable pattern of income so that it can forecast whether the school should expect expanding or contracting resources (assuming that the GSB will be increased approximately in line with pay and price rises).

With the Development Plan in mind, they should list the proposed changes and then estimate the resource implications of the various means of bringing about those changes. The school can then predict the most likely alternatives and identify how these will affect the resource demands in the various budget headings.

There is no need yet to eliminate all those activities which the school will probably be unable to fund. It is a good business maxim that organisations should plan to spend 105% and then make choices between different alternatives to bring spending down to 100%. This enhances creativity by expanding possible choices. In contrast, organisations which are very cautious usually plan 95% expenditure and keep contingency funds. This latter approach is very constraining and tends to result in organisations being budget-led.

3. Budgetary Implementation – Drawing up the Final Budget

The nature of the local government finance system means that funds are allocated to education just before the new financial year begins. However, schools should not wait until this stage before considering allocation to budget headings. Many LEAs are producing details of provisional budgets and, unless the political climate is very unstable, it is worth planning allocations based on this information.

The stages of the budget implementation process are:

- check the provisional delegated budget for accuracy:
- set out headings and sub-headings as supplied by the LEA;
- allocate fixed costs (eg rates, phone rental) to headings;
- allocate recurrent expenditure based on last year's information (if it was accurate and an effective use of funds);
- look at the budgetary review and forecast in order to see priorities for development;
- decide between alternative projects and courses of action;

- leave a list of 'unfunded priorities' should further funds become available (through virement or fundraising) later in the year;
- receive final figures from the LEA;
- make the necessary adjustments;
- approve the budget document at a governors' meeting;
- staff can then place orders and administrative staff can deal with deliveries, contracts and so on;
- as the year progresses, monitoring may reveal opportunities for virement;
- evaluate areas of expenditure for effectiveness (see below);
- prepare reports on expenditure – in the interim these will be for governors' meetings but, once a year, the information will be made available to the parents through their annual meeting with the governors.

4. Budgetary Evaluation

It is important that schools do not neglect the evaluation of the budgetary process; this stage focuses on the effectiveness of the process and may suggest improvements in the future. The main purpose of the evaluation should be to consider how well targets and objectives have been resourced. However, it is also important to evaluate the process by which this resourcing took place by considering the role of the partners in the process and the timescale of the activities.

THE PEOPLE DIMENSION

It is important to consider not only the distribution of the funds but also how the allocations are decided. Staff and governors need to be clear who is involved and who makes the final decisions. There should be no confusion about the extent of consultation or actual participation in the decision-making process. Although the focus of this chapter has been on the stages in the budget development process, there has been reference to the participants in the process. Chapter 5 goes on to consider how the partners can work together effectively without giving up large amounts of their valuable time.

5
The Role of Governors, Head and Staff in the Budgetary Process

The Education Reform Act gives considerable powers to governing bodies to facilitate the Local Management of Schools. Amongst these powers are the right to determine policy and make decisions in a number of areas. The reasoning behind this move to greater autonomy is that the governors are able to make more effective decisions because they are closer to the pupils than a more remotely sited LEA. Nevertheless, the DES envisages '... that in practice much of the detailed control over expenditure and the day to day running of the school will be delegated by the governing body to the headteacher' (DES Circular 7/88). Individual governing bodies will decide for themselves how far to devolve powers to the head, depending on their judgement of local circumstances.

DES guidelines then turn to the role of the head; they state that 'the headteacher will have a key role in helping the governing body to formulate a management plan for the school, and in securing its implementation with the collective support of the staff.' Good management practice would suggest that there should be considerable staff involvement in preparing the School Management Development Plan and in the associated resource decisions. The staff are, after all, even closer to the clients than are the governors. This would allow staff to feel committed to the proposed activities and to the means of achieving them.

If governors, heads and staff are to work together effectively there is a need to clarify their roles and responsibilities as partners in the school. This chapter examines how this can be made more effective in order to enhance the quality of school management.

THE STRUCTURE OF POLICY MAKING

In order to fulfil its legal responsibilities, each governing body must have written policies for certain aspects of the school such as the curriculum and collective worship. The policy process involves the four activities of generation, approval, implementation and administration.

It is useful to analyse the various roles of the partners in the school in each of these four activities. Do the governors simply approve or veto policy recommendations passed on to them by the professionals — or do they actually take part in the policy review and generation process? Each school will have to work out its own framework and relationships with governors to manage this. Similarly, staff in the school may just be carrying out policy laid down by the governors and head but they will have greater commitment and enthusiasm if they take part in generating the policy from the outset.

Policy administration should largely be carried out by support staff, so it may be helpful to consider some involvement at earlier stages so that they too understand the background to their work.

In assessing the role of the governors, head and staff in managing LMS four levels of activity can be identified:

- Policy approval
- Policy generation
- Policy implementation
- Policy administration

If governors are to fulfil their role how can the school management cycle be set up to facilitate a positive contribution to school management? The experience to date of many new primary school governors has been disappointing. Taking an interest and making a commitment has often resulted in frustration at interminably long meetings which concentrate on legal and formal requirements from the LEA with little time actually being spent on issues that seem directly related to children and the learning process. How then can we ensure that the relationship between governors, heads and staff becomes a productive one? Initially we will look at a more effective way of organising governor involvement.

THE ROLE OF GOVERNORS

Three factors must be foremost in establishing a good working relationship with the school:

1. governors need to develop a broader and more detailed understanding of schools and what goes on in them;

2. finance should be seen in the context of the wider education-led process;
3. the amount of time which governors and staff can commit to meetings is very limited.

It is difficult to encompass all this within the historical pattern of three governors' meetings per term. One solution is to have a series of governors' sub-committees which deal with such matters as finance, curriculum, staffing, premises, marketing and so on. The major disadvantage is that it fragments decision-making areas which are closely linked. In a primary school it would seem to be a very retrograde step, for example, if finance were to be discussed in isolation from the curriculum. A further problem arises with sub-committees in that some of the governors would have a great deal of knowledge and power while others would have relatively little.

What is needed is for the governors to separate out the 'business' part of their task and the 'school policy' part of their task. This is also a good approach in general terms for staff meetings: it is valuable to separate into two different meetings those issues which are of a routine and administrative nature and those which involve, for example, a major review of the curriculum. A central feature of this approach is that while business meetings may have a number of items and take a long time, school policy discussions should be focused on one major item for review and last for a defined amount of time, preferably one hour. A 'one hour one issue meeting' is a valuable management approach for concentrating efforts on a major area of policy. A further consideration is that the role of the governors should not be seen in isolation from that of the staff of the school. A system needs to be established which integrates staff, the headteacher and the governors in a partnership. What follows is a framework which encompasses these perspectives.

The Proposed Pattern of Governor Involvement
An alternative framework can be established to build on the existing pattern of full governors' meetings and to link this with the internal school structure. The pattern of governors' meetings traditionally has been one per term:

(1) - (3) Existing governors' meetings

In operating LMS, with one meeting per term in the traditional pattern, the meeting before Easter would review the financial plans while the one after Easter, when the financial allocation was known from the LEA, would formally approve the budget. In the Autumn Term the meeting would concern itself with monitoring and proposing any virement, as would the Spring Term meeting.

Parallel to this would be the system of internal staff committees and working parties on curriculum, pastoral care, discipline, distribution of capitation and, more recently, marketing.

The internal committees will need to have a termly progress review meeting where staff update the governors on policy developments and engage them in a discussion as to the desirability and viability of the various options. This would have two purposes; firstly, it would integrate the governors with the internal school management and, secondly, it would provide them with an information base on which to make decisions. The nature of these meetings would be about an hour on curriculum or other issues with staff and governors together and then the second part taking the form of a normal governors' meeting.

The minimum pattern envisaged would be:

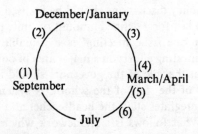

Autumn Term:
(1) governors' meeting including financial monitoring report.
(2) curriculum review/governors' business.

Spring Term:
(3) pastoral care review/governors' business.
(4) governors' meeting/budget planning and policy.

Summer Term:
(5) governors' meeting/budget approval.
(6) external relations and marketing review/governors' business.

Curriculum discussions thus come before budget discussions so that they can inform them and set them in an educational context. This does not mean that there would not be other meetings, for example, dealing with the appointment of staff or responding to the rising flood of government policy documents and initiatives, or that governors will not have to look at property and other issues. What it does do is to set up a framework in which policy formulation and discussion prioritises staff/governor interaction and does not leave governors merely rubber-stamping school decisions.

Although not all governors are able to attend all meetings, this level of activity is necessary if the role of the governor is to be one of an informed partner in the relationship between staff, governors and the LEA. Also, it should involve all governors so that collectively they are aware of issues and can have an informed view.

Team and Task Groups vs Standing Committees

Undoubtedly, as mentioned above, there will be times when sub-groups will have to meet. The danger of permanent committees is that they separate out what we see as the integrated nature of curriculum, staffing and financial decisions. If all governors have developed a broader view of the school by the six meeting pattern, additional tasks could be tackled by specific sub-groups.

These would have a single task (eg the next year's budget), a defined reporting span, and would then be disbanded. This enables focus and specific task orientation yet avoids permanent sub-committees taking root.

The composition of these temporary groups should represent available expertise both in terms of technical knowledge and of the skills necessary for effective and relevant outcomes. They should not just be microcosms of the main body nor should issues of status compromise the ability of the group to solve problems and generate policies. Given the limited life span of such groups, it is essential that they are trained to work effectively in order to achieve the task.

THE ROLE OF STAFF

It was stated earlier that if decision-making is delegated *to* schools because they are closer to the children and are better able to make decisions for the resource needs of children then the same argument can be applied *within* schools. Should delegation stop at the level of the governors and head? Or should allowance-holders and main professional grade teachers, because they are in day to day contact with the children, be involved in determining spending? As these staff can judge the needs of the children in their care there is clearly a role for them in the decision-making process when it comes to resourcing those needs. If staff are not to see LMS as a threat they need to be involved in the benefits which flexibility brings. This means involving them in determining needs, setting priorities and making choices between those priorities. In terms of the policy stages listed on page 50 they should contribute to the policy generation stage as well as the policy implementation stage. The extent and organisation of this consultation and/or participation is for each school to determine. The following framework is recommended to the reader to provide a means of assessing the response to this question of staff involvement in his or her school.

Participation Framework

Assess the appropriate degree of consultation and participation of allowance holders and main professional grade teachers in deciding budgetary expenditure in the following areas:

Teachers
    Full-time
    Part-time
    Supply
	Books and Materials
	Educational Equipment
	Reprographics
	School visits

Assistants Full-time	Equipment rental
Part-time	Furniture
Clerical Full-time	Classroom Fittings
Part-time	Classroom Maintenance
Professional Development	Others

Identify the reasons for the judgements you make on individual items.

THE ROLE OF THE HEADTEACHER

It was stated earlier that the government, in its legislation, envisages that the detailed control over expenditure and the day to day running of the school will be delegated by the governing body to the headteacher. This can only happen in the context of a management plan for the school. The previous chapter examined the importance of establishing a School Management Development Plan. This then will be the key task for a headteacher so that budgetary decisions can be set in the context of the whole school and its aims and objectives. The new skills which headteachers will require, and the effect on their leadership style in this new framework, will be considerable. Although the skills which they will need are numerous, what follows is a list that should clarify for the reader some of the budgetary skills:

- **Understanding** - the nature of the formula, how the school budget share is determined and the school budget is structured.

- **Assessing** - establishing priorities and comparing alternatives and costs.

- **Consulting** - with governors, staff and all others affected.

- **Deciding** - which policies and priorities to implement, when and how.

- **Recording** - the decisions about the budget and laying down agreed procedures and responsibilities to ensure that there is no confusion about role or decision.

- **Evaluating** - whether adjustments and changes in spending allocations have improved the quality of education for the children in the school.

The changes in the leadership style and approach of the headteacher in the LMS framework can be considered from several points of view:

1. a greater emphasis on the *managerial* role; management is about 'getting things done through people', and heads will have to concern themselves with organising others and delegating and not simply being the leading professional and leading by example.

2. a more *participatory* and *consultative* decision-making approach in order to involve governors and staff in school decisions to develop a team approach with governors and staff.

3. greater accountability and responsibility in the field of LMS means that greater *communication* and explanation of decisions is required.

4. an assessment of whether or not the increased role of the governors results in the head moving towards becoming a chief executive reporting to a board of directors!

THE NEED TO RE-ASSESS RELATIONSHIPS IN AN LMS SCHOOL

It is important that schools consider not only the financial and technical aspects of LMS but also the relationships between the people involved in the process. Historically it has always been a mistake in Europe to fight a war on two fronts. With LMS if schools are struggling with both the operation of LMS and the ill-defined role of the people involved, success may be jeopardised. It is important therefore to establish the roles of staff, the head and the governors and their working relationship before the technicalities of LMS are tackled. If they function as a team with a clear understanding of their contribution to the process there should be a better chance of success.

This chapter has examined the roles and relationships of the people involved in managing LMS. The next four chapters use a case study approach to examine the stages through which a school will need to go when operating its budget.

6
Case Study Outline: Brentwich School

This chapter and the following three will establish details about a typical primary school and illustrate the sequence of events that form the budgetary process.

This chapter sets the scene and gives basic information about the case study school; the succeeding three take the reader step by step through the key budgetary stages of *review, forecasting* and *implementation*. At each of these stages a framework for analysing the budgetary process will be established and a model solution presented. We hope that the reader will then be able to replicate this process in his or her own school and that it will make a contribution to the establishment of good budgetary practice.

THE CASE STUDY SCHOOL

In order to enable the reader to work through the stages in the budgetary process we first need to establish information about a typical primary school. The following material about 'Brentwich School' aims to provide this context and is structured in five major categories:

1. Background information about the school (p.58)
2. Staffing information (p.59)
3. Curriculum review reports (p.63)
4. Physical resources and support services review (p.69)
5. Information regarding the pupil roll and budget (p.71)

To take the reader through the case study material it is envisaged that the reader was appointed to the headship of the school on 1st May 1990 and is trying to grapple with the complexities of LMS and the leadership requirements of the new post.

1. BACKGROUND INFORMATION ABOUT THE SCHOOL

Brentwich School is a traditional Group 5 (new Group 2) primary school for about 287 children aged 5–11. It is situated in a predominantly middle class area with extensive private housing near the school. Approximately 25 per cent of the intake come from the industrial part of the town drawn from a more mixed housing stock.

The market town has grown up as a significant commuter base for travelling into the nearby urban conurbation. There are good motorway links and considerable light industry and technology-based firms nearby. Extensive growth in the service sector of the economy has also led to expansion in this area of local employment.

There are limited community links which could be expanded and developed. Currently the school allows a local playgroup to use the hall on two mornings per week. There is no adult education use of the building. The governors' policy on lettings indicates their lack of awareness or interest in this area.

In the immediate vicinity there are two other 5-11 schools, one a new purpose-built county school and the other a voluntary aided school. There is a private preparatory school five miles away and a private nursery school in the town. Competition for pupils out of the traditional catchment areas is becoming a key factor. In the term before transfer the children visit the comprehensive school to which they will transfer.

The school has a uniform policy which recommends a school sweatshirt and grey trousers/skirt. Most pupils comply with this. The voluntary aided school has a traditional tie and blazer uniform for both boys and girls.

The school was built in the early 1960s on traditional lines with individual classrooms. The internal part of the school was redecorated four years ago. Externally the school has pleasant grounds with its own sports facilities.

The staff of the school consists of the Head and 11.9 full-time staff equivalents. The staff contact with parents is based on parents' evenings and limited contact with the PTA which is semi-dormant.

The previous headteacher had been appointed in 1967 and had firm views about the way in which the school should be led. Concerned that the school would receive a delegated budget in April 1990, she took early retirement at Christmas 1989. Since then the deputy head has been the acting head. However, the acting head was not very confident about finance and the new chairman of governors (a local estate agent) has taken charge of the budget.

The school aims were produced last term by the acting head because he felt that the existing statement was very out of date. However, they were then stored in his briefcase! It appears that the staff and governors are unaware of their content and that, therefore, the chairman of governors did not refer to them when preparing the budget. This statement of aims begins:

'The school aims to provide a caring environment which offers a broad and balanced curriculum to promote the intellectual, spiritual, moral, cultural, social and physical development of pupils. This will prepare them for the opportunities, responsibilities and experience of life in a rapidly changing world. Great emphasis is placed on developing the abilities and talents of each individual.' Wherever possible these aims are achieved through an integrated approach to the curriculum so that knowledge, skills and attitudes are conveyed in a meaningful way.

2. STAFFING INFORMATION

Staff Profiles

Full Time	Scale	Date of appointment
Mr Hope (39) BA(OU), BEd (Hons), Advanced Dip in Primary Ed.	Headteacher (Group 5)	1/5/90
Mr Day (33) BEd (Hons), DPSE Years 2/3	Deputy Head (Group 5)	1/9/87
Mrs Maxwell (41) Senior Management Team BEd (Hons), CertEd Years 1/2	PT 11 + B allowance (mathematics)	1/9/82
Miss Saunders (46) Senior Management Team BSc, PGCE, Advanced Dip in Primary Sceience Years 3/4	Pt 11 + B allowance (science)	1/9/87
Miss Robson (39) BEd (Hons) (Early Years) Year R (reception)	Pt 7 + A allowance (display)	1/4/88

Mrs Underwood (57) CertEd Close friend of previous head Year 5	Pt 11 + A allowance (looking after the reading scheme)	1/9/71
Mrs Elkins (39) CertEd No class - just returned to teaching after career break; started InService B Ed in September 1989	Pt 9	1/9/89
Miss Farmer (24) BEd (Hons) Year 6	Pt 4 (Probationer)	1/9/89
Mrs Goddard (37) BA(OU), CertEd returned to full-time teaching after career break and supply work Year 2	Pt 10	1/4/87
Miss Ingram (32) BA (English and Media Studies), PGCE Year 4. Previously a journalist	Pt 8	1/9/88
Mrs Nolan (44) CertEd Class R/1	Pt 10	1/9/84
Mr Pilkington (25) BEd(PE) Year 5/6	Pt 5	1/9/88

Part Time

Mrs Allen (35) CertEd, DPSE (Special Educational Needs in the Mainstream School). 0.3 Special Needs Permanent contract	Pt 9	1/1/85
Mrs Black (30) BA(Hons), CertEd, LRAM 0.4 Plays the piano Temporary contract – renewed annually to date	Pt 9	1/9/86

Mrs Carter (35)   Pt 7   1/9/88
CertEd
0.2 temporary contract
Officially intended to share
the Deputy's class to allow
 him time for management
– the previous head felt
that this was unnecessary
so she acts as a support
teacher as required. During
the term when the deputy
was acting head, she was full
time and a supply teacher
came in to do the 0.2 post.

*All allowances are permanent   ** Pt = point on the incremental scale.
NB. Throughout this case study 'Main Professional Grade' is used as this will
be familiar to the reader. However, as time progresses the new term 'Standard
National Scale' will become more widely recognised.

Teaching Staff Salaries
NB. For simplicity's sake it has been assumed that 'on costs' are
15.5% of gross salary for everyone except Mrs Carter who only pays
National Insurance (7%).

Name	FTE	(£) Full Year Cost*		
		At 1/4/90	At 1/9/90	At 1/1/91
Mr Hope	1.0	24587.64	24587.64	25294.50
Mr Day	1.0	21292.43	21292.43	22176.00
Mrs Maxwell	1.0	19764.36	19764.36	20212.50
Miss Saunders	1.0	19764.36	19764.36	20212.50
Miss Robson	1.0	15508.19	16374.44	16374.44
Mrs Underwood	1.0	19230.75	19230.75	19550.69
Miss Farmer	1.0	11604.29	12567.56	12705.00
Mrs Goddard	1.0	17207.19	18160.07	18480.00
Miss Ingram	1.0	15303.75	16170.00	16170.00
Mrs Elkins	1.0	16170.00	17207.19	17325.00
Mrs Nolan	1.0	17207.19	18160.07	18480.00
Mr Pilkington	1.0	12567.56	13571.25	13571.25
Mrs Allen	0.3	4851.00	5162.16	5197.50
Mrs Black	0.4	6468.00	6882.88	6930.00
Mrs Carter	0.2	2675.00	2835.50	2835.50

*The 1990/91 teachers' pay award was in two parts, the first in April
1990 and the second in January 1991 (although some points on the
scale were unaffected by the latter adjustment).

In addition those teachers who are below Point 11 on the scale have an annual increment in September.

The figures in the three main columns above give the full annual cost of the salary at that particular time. However, the actual cost to the school for the year 1990/91 would be 5/12 the cost in April + 4/12 the cost in September + 3/12 the cost in January = £229,538.45.

Non-Teaching Staff

| | (£) Full Year Cost | |
	1/4/90	1/7/90*
Mrs King (25 hrs) Temporary Classroom assistant	5,017.00	5,318.02
Mrs Tell (25 hrs) School Secretary	5,289.00	5,659.23
Mrs Wordsworth (22 hrs) Clerical Assistant	4,416.00	4,725.12
Mrs Orwell (12 hrs) Administrative Officer (LMS)	3,959.00	4,236.13
Mr Jordan (39 hrs) Caretaker	9,180.00**	9,822.60**
Midday Supervisors 6.25 hrs:		
Mrs Lucas	776.28	830.62
Mrs Law	776.28	830.62
Mrs Lowndes	776.28	830.62
Mrs Lillee	776.28	830.62
Mrs Lewis	754.62	807.44
Mrs Senior	1,425.24	1,525.01

*Assuming 6% pay rise in July
**This can be increased by a 15% bonus rate.

The figures in the two main columns above give the full annual cost of the salary at that particular time. However, the actual cost to the school for the year 1990/91 would be 3/12 of the cost in April + 9/12 of the cost in July.

NB. Only Mr Jordan pays superannuation – the rest just pay National Insurance.

3. CURRICULUM REVIEW REPORTS

In order to acquire the information which you need to carry out the 'Budgetary Review' (see page 75), you have asked individuals and teams of staff to report on the following areas of the curriculum:

Mathematics	Art
English (including Drama)	Music
Science	PE and Dance
Technology	RE
History & Geography	
Personal, Social & Health Education	
Special Needs	

Your request for this review was made on 23rd May and you have asked for responses by 23rd July. The responses are given below.

Mathematics
This review was prepared by Mrs Maxwell (mathematics co-ordinator), Miss Ingram and Mr Pilkington.

The aim of our work in this area is to develop mathematical skills and understanding through practical tasks and real life situations. In the early years this is achieved in a less formal way than in the later years.

A new scheme was introduced in September 1988 in the reception class and this ties in quite well with the requirements of the National Curriculum. Supplementary activities have been provided where needed. Resources to support the scheme have been assembled and are stored in classrooms. The resources are therefore readily available and are well maintained by staff. They are checked termly by the maths co-ordinator.

Staff development has taken place (a training day and five one-hour workshops) and those not yet using the scheme have experienced it by inter-visiting, both within school (as this helps continuity) and with other schools (so that they have wider access to ideas and have seen the scheme in use with their 'own' age group).

Future needs in this area
1. To integrate IT more carefully into the scheme rather than it being 'bolt on'. We need to look more carefully at IT in National Curriculum maths and at aspects of Technology (AT5).

2. To produce a checksheet showing which aspects of National Curriculum maths are covered by the publisher's scheme and which by supplementary activities or by topic work in other areas of the curriculum. The preparation of this checksheet is already underway. It has been completed for Key Stage 1.

3. To further develop the record keeping system for individual pupils.

4. To consider continuity with nursery provision and at 11.

5. To keep parents informed as the scheme moves up the school and to consider the introduction of 'Shared Maths'.

English
This review should have been prepared by Mrs Underwood, Mrs Nolan and Mrs Elkins. In the event, Mrs Nolan was ill and Mrs Underwood felt that it was a pointless exercise, so Mrs Elkins did it on her own following visits to similar schools in the next town.

The aim of our work in this area is to encourage all forms of communication and to develop self-expression. Language is seen as an integral part of all school activities and this leads to monitoring complications in respect of the National Curriculum.

The reading scheme is looking dated – it is not very good on equal opportunity (especially gender and race), the books are getting 'tatty' and they are not very exciting or interesting. Similar criticisms can be made about supplementary readers which need to be more inviting.

The Library has a reasonable stock of reference material, is well laid out, and the readers for older children are adequate as a grant was received last year.

The only home-school link with regard to language is that reading books are sent home at the weekend. Most staff assume that in this town parents are well-motivated and are able to back up the work at home.

A school newspaper has been developed by the older pupils, largely through the initiative of Miss Ingram who has expertise in the area of IT and who used to work for the local newspaper. A parent is also giving some assistance with this project. It is proposed that the pupils will interview members of local industry during the coming year.

Future needs in this area

1. To develop a whole new policy on language, prioritising reading and adopting a new scheme.

2. To increase parental links such as shared reading, both at home and in school.

3. To improve the supply of stimulating supplementary readers.

4. In the light of the National Curriculum, to review the access to reference material for individual work – possibly considering the devolution of some funds to classroom libraries.

5. To include work from lower down the school in the newspaper and, later, to enable younger pupils to develop a broadsheet themselves. Work in this area needs to be tied in with aspects of the National Curriculum (Technology as well as English).

Science
This review was prepared by Miss Saunders (science co-ordinator), Mrs King (classroom assistant) and Mrs Goddard.

The school has always done a lot of environmental science such as nature study and keeping animals. A science co-ordinator was appointed in September 1987 and since then there has been a gradual move (throughout the school) to wider content and a process based investigative approach.

The science scheme was developed 'in-house' and has been modified to encompass the National Curriculum. The scheme is well documented. Resources are all adequate if used carefully and replaced correctly. They are regularly checked by Mrs King.

Extensive staff development has taken place, comprising INSET from the co-ordinator and a visiting lecturer (in the form of workshops, classroom support, material preparation, shared ideas, inter-visiting).

Future needs in this area:

1. We would like to have a visiting 'scientist' (in the same way as there are visiting artists and poets).

2. Closer links could be developed with technology.

3. In order to cover the extensive requirements of National Curriculum Science we may have to consider the balance between cross-curricular approaches and purely 'science' projects. If the latter proves necessary, attention could be given to aspects of other National Curriculum areas which could be monitored during science projects.

4. Although resourcing has been extensive over the last few years, there are yet further needs if statutory obligations are to be met.

5. The record-keeping system needs to be further developed.

6. There needs to be greater liaison with the comprehensive school in order to ensure continuity.

Technology
Report prepared by deputy head (to try to clarify the situation in this area), Miss Ingram and Mrs Allen.

This is an area where staff lack expertise and confidence. This area of the curriculum has not developed, despite an LEA support team being available.

Individual class teachers have been encouraged to consider how technology in the National Curriculum is covered by their existing project work and then to add areas which are still missing. Resources are not co-ordinated, each member of staff is expected to find his/her own. There is one computer in each classroom.

Miss Ingram attended a 2-day course and reported back to staff at an end of term meeting.

Future needs in this area:

1. To appoint a co-ordinator and to encourage someone else to be an ally in the change process.

2. To develop a well documented scheme with adequate resources – projects, worksheets, etc in order to give a framework, varied equipment, kits, tools, materials. There will need to be some attempt to acquire resources from parents and industry. Resources will need suitable storage places and a member of staff will have to monitor the use and availability of the resources.

3. To instigate considerable staff development – extensive workshops and classroom support needed to increase skills, knowledge and

confidence in order to secure the implementation of good practice.

History & Geography

This statement was prepared by the deputy head – there was no need for a task group.

Provision in these areas is very ad hoc. There are no subject co-ordinators. Staff include them in projects as they see fit – very much depends on their own interests and knowledge.

Future needs in these areas:

1. To appoint a co-ordinator.

2. To examine the proposals for National Curriculum History and Geography as they emerge.

3. To analyse the extent to which these appear in the work of the school and to develop the means of implementing the statutory orders when available.

Art

Prepared by Miss Robson (in charge of display), Miss Farmer and Mrs Carter.

There is good quality display throughout the school as there is a co-ordinated approach, although the time and cost of double mounting is causing concern.

In the pupils' work there is a good balance of two and three dimensional areas and a wide range of skills are developed. The staff seem to have a lot of expertise in this area.

Future needs in this area:

1. To put up more displays in the community eg the local library.

2. To enable another visiting artist to work in the school – the last one was in 1986.

Music

This review was prepared by Mrs Black (part-time teacher who plays the piano), Miss Robson and the Head (who sings in a choir).

The music specialist left during the previous academic year. Other staff feel that they do not have the necessary skills because they cannot sing or play an instrument. Mrs Black plays the piano and this therefore constrains 'timetabling'. The curriculum is limited to class singing, listening to music and, for some, learning traditional instruments.

Future needs in this area:

1. Designate or appoint a member of staff to be responsible for developing the music curriculum and provide the necessary INSET for this person.

2. Ensure that there is greater continuity in the curriculum and an emphasis on less formal 'music making' for all.

3. Introduce technology into the music curriculum.

4. Instigate a programme of staff development so that every member of staff has the skills and confidence to deliver the curriculum to his/her own class.

PE and Dance
This review was prepared by Mr Pilkington (PE specialist), Mrs Maxwell and the LEA dance coordinator.

There is a coherent programme in place which develops physical skills and team building. Most staff feel able to deal with this area but specialist staffing is available if anyone wants to 'swap'.

The school is fortunate that an ex-member of staff is the LEA coordinator and she therefore spends quite a lot of time supporting staff.

Future needs in this area:

1. To be less reliant on the LEA and to develop dance expertise amongst the staff.

2. In the long term to look towards the National Curriculum.

RE
This review was prepared by the head, the deputy chairman of governors (a lay preacher who expressed specific interest in this area) and Miss Saunders.

The school is meeting the requirements of the Education Reform Act in that there is a daily collective act of worship. This is of a Christian nature and takes various forms in a week – either whole school, infant, junior or individual class. Other aspects of RE are picked up in topic work according to the teacher's preference.

Personal, Social and Health Education
The deputy head reports that this area has not been given any consideration by the school but that he believes that an effort should be made to examine these issues in a cross-curricular way.

Special Needs
This report was prepared by Mrs Allen.

Despite the existence of a policy on Special Needs, the school seems to believe that there are few problems in this respect and low priority is given to meeting the needs of the 20% of children who have learning difficulties at some stage in their school career.

Future needs in this area:

1. More effort should be made to consider the needs of individuals and to identify and remedy individual problems. I attempt to do this but because I am only available for part of the week there seems to be little impact on the school as a whole.

2. There is a need to support staff in identifying problems and tackling them within the classroom rather than, as now, splitting classes to make life easier for the teacher in charge.

3. There is also a need to look at the experiences being offered to the most able pupils, especially as they move up the school and operate at a different National Curriculum level to their peers.

4. PHYSICAL RESOURCES AND SUPPORT SERVICES REVIEW

As a temporary arrangement, you have asked a team to conduct a review of the physical resources within the school. This team comprises a parent governor (who is a builder), the deputy head and the caretaker. Similarly, the office and support staff have been asked to review their areas to highlight any particular problems.

Physical Resources Report

The *entrance hall* has some loose floor tiles and the whole area gives a poor first image of the school. The pictures on the wall are very old and the plants are straggly. There are no chairs for people who are waiting. These points were noted by Mr Vickers (governor) while he was waiting for the first meeting.

With our present class structure, there are enough *classrooms* and we have one spare for the library. Problems arise within classrooms when the pupils are undertaking major practical activities because the rooms are not big enough to have a designated 'practical area'.

The whole school was *decorated* in 1986. We need to consider the rolling programme of redecoration. Mr Vickers has contacts in this area. A suggestion is that we start with the rooms used by the older children and work downwards. Staff should have some involvement in the 'decor'.

All the *furniture* was new ten years ago and here again forward planning for replacement will be important. The only major needs at the moment seem to be trolleys for moveable storage, filing cabinets for the staff and blinds for the office (to prevent sun streaming onto the computer screen).

Routine *maintenance* seems to be running smoothly. Minor repairs have been carried out quickly and effectively by registered glaziers and plumbers.

Externally, we have little responsibility but some areas would warrant further consideration.

1. The school sign is very dilapidated. It gives a very poor image.

2. The low brick wall between the garden and the playground is losing mortar. Mr Vickers believes that failure to attend to this could result in bricks becoming loose and the possibility of accidents to pupils.

3. The caretaker has noticed that there is little for the children to do at lunchtimes. Perhaps we could consider some playground markings and some apparatus.

Office/Support Services Report

The office staff are concerned about the fact that no one is available to answer the telephone during their lunchtime (12 until 1) or late in the day (after 3 pm). They are also unclear about their individual roles and responsibilities, eg staff are increasingly handing in items to be wordprocessed but Mrs Wordsworth feels that this is not part of her job.

Problems are experienced when using the computer because the sun shines in during the morning. This has been mentioned to the team looking at physical resources.

There is a dearth of information which can be given or sent out to people enquiring about the school and there is uncertainty about where to 'put' visitors who are waiting to see staff.

Mrs King feels that staff value her assistance but she is finding it very difficult to respond to all the requests for assistance, especially now that she is spending so much time cutting up paper for display.

5. INFORMATION REGARDING THE PUPIL ROLL AND BUDGET

Pupil Roll

The LEA has sent the following information about the Form 7 figures, confirming the actual numbers which the acting head supplied and giving the LEA's estimate of future trends.

Age at 31/8	NC YrGp	Jan 1990 Actual	Jan 1991 Proj.	Jan 1992 Proj.	Jan 1993 Proj.	Jan 1994 Proj.
10	6	42	41	41	37	50
9	5	41	41	37	50	33
8	4	41	37	50	33	43
7	3	37	50	33	43	40
6	2	50	33	43	40	38
5	1	33	43	40	38	34
4	R	43	40	38	34	36
FTE		287	285	282	275	274

NB. The school takes rising fives in September and January.

Roll for the School – January 1990

In order to calculate much of the income to the school, the LEA weights pupils according to age (see page 72) based entirely on the previous January's Form 7. The case study LEA weights infants at 1 and Juniors at 1.05. The age weighted pupil units are thus calculated as follows:

Pupil age	Pupil Numbers	Weighting	AWPU
10	42		
9	41		
8	41	× 1.05	= 169.05
7	37		
6	50		
5	33	× 1.00	= 126
4	43		

Total pupil numbers = 287
Total Age Weighted Pupil Units (AWPU)   = 295.05

The formula and the School Budget
The LEA formula is divided into two parts:

A. The aggregated age weighted pupil part – which is calculated by multiplying the pupil unit of resource by the school's AWPU total.

B. The other factors part – in the case study school these factors comprise:

1. Curriculum and Small School Protection as follows:

(a) Small School Subsidy – 0.12 of a unit of resource for the difference between the actual roll and 360 pupils.

(b) Flat rate allocation – 58 units of resource for each primary school.

(c) A management allowance of 6 units of resource to provide for the extra administrative load of managing LMS.

2. Premises Related Factors as follows:

(a) Floor area of buildings (in square metres) which is then multiplied by the funding per square metre.

(b) Area of grounds (in hectares) which is then multiplied by the funding per hectare.

(c) Rates which are funded at actual cost.

3. Special Needs funding calculated according to the LEA's formula for pupil support and incidence of social deprivation.

The way in which this works out in the case study school can be seen on the following page:

SCHOOL BUDGET FOR THE YEAR 1990/91

Income Budget

A. Aggregated Age Weighted Pupil Units × Pupil Unit of Resource
   AWPU Current Year = 295.05 × £804 =   £237,220

B.   1. *Other Factors*
                                    Units
      Small school allowance
      360 – NOR = 73
      therefore   73 × 0.12 =   8.76
      Flat rate allowance   58.00
      LMS allowance   6.00

      Total units =   72.76
      Total Units × Other Factors Unit of Resource
      72.76 units × £764 =   £ 55,589

      2. *Premises Formula*
      (a) Floor area × funding per square metre
          $1523m^2$ × £4.77   £ 7,265
      (b) Grounds × funding per hectare
          1.49 hect × £3789.85 =   £ 5,647
      (c) Rates   £12,831
                                             = £ 25,743

      3. *Special Needs Formula Funding*   = £ 2,533

      Formula Budget Total =   **£321,085**

Expenditure Budget for 1990/91

As drawn up by the Chairman of Governors

Staffing	£	£
Teaching Staff	229,538	
Admin & Support Staff	19,624	
Midday Supervision	5,562	
Caretaking	11,111	
Supply	4,128	
Duty Meals	1,500	
		271,463
Premises		
Building Maintenance	5,667	
Energy	7,615	
Rates (Fixed Amount)	12,831	
Grounds Maintenance	5,139	
Other Premises	2,310	
(Water rates, sewerage etc)		33,562
General Expenses		
Supplies & Services	12,560	
School Improvements	2,000	
Advertising	500	
Contingency	1,000	
		16,060
Planned Expenditure Total		**321,085**

UNDERTAKING THE THREE BUDGETARY STAGES

The next three chapters take the reader through the following stages:

1. Starting in the Summer Term, a *review* of the existing pattern of activities and resources to determine areas for development. This process is demonstrated in Chapter 7.

2. Later in the year (second half of the Autumn Term) a *forecasting* or forward planning exercise looking at trends over the next three years (Chapter 8).

3. In the Spring Term a *budgetary implementation* process for the new financial year (Chapter 9).

7
Case Study Area One: Budgetary Review

The budgetary review will examine the main areas of the school which are based on the current year's practice. This involves assessing current spending patterns and producing a list of priorities for consideration. This chapter therefore, will replicate good practice and produce the following key information:

1. an outline of the major curriculum needs and priorities that arise from the curriculum review;

2. the priorities for consideration in the area of staffing;

3. items for urgent consideration emerging from the review of physical resources;

4. a statement of any changes deemed desirable in the relationship with the local community.

BUDGETARY REVIEW PART 1: CURRICULUM

The need for major curriculum development in an area should be stated here and an outline given of the nature of the need, ie equipment, books, materials, storage. There will also be other curricular areas which seem to need some support, although to a lesser extent.

This section draws on the perspectives in Chapter Four and the information about Brentwich School in Chapter Six.

The school already has a statement of aims and the initial data collection in the curriculum area suggests that Science, PE and Art give no major cause for concern. However, it would seem that management attention is needed in the following areas:

- The statement of aims needs to be agreed by the whole school, clearly articulated and published.

- A language policy must be developed. This will have resource implications when changes such as a new reading scheme are adopted, the infant library books are supplemented and the curriculum co-ordinator post is reviewed. There will also be a need to change attitudes to reading and to enhance the role of parents.

- A curriculum policy for Technology is required as a matter of urgency. This will involve staff time and a need to set aside resources for equipment and materials. The problem of suitable space in classrooms for practical work is highlighted in the 'Physical Resources' review.

- History and Geography must be developed in line with National Curriculum legislation. This is likely to create new resource demands in terms of materials and staff development.

- The whole area of Special Needs provision requires higher priority.

- Music has staffing problems and operates a narrow curriculum which needs restructuring.

- In Maths a new approach has been established successfully in the early years, but if this adoption is to be spread more quickly to the juniors, then extra materials will be required.

- Personal, Social and Health Education and Religious Education need a curriculum policy and resource costing.

As well as this examination of policy, the initial analysis of the budget drawn up by the Chairman of Governors reveals that National Curriculum demands are likely to lead to a £1,000 overspend on the capitation part of the supplies and services element of the budget.

BUDGETARY REVIEW PART 2: STAFFING

This section relates to both teaching and non-teaching staff and so draws together information from the staffing and support services reviews. The statement of priorities will define existing areas of expertise and areas in need of development. This involves a consideration of the existence and effectiveness of curriculum co-ordinators and areas where recruitment and retention are required. In order to make the best use of current staff it will be necessary to highlight areas where staff development or succession planning is required.

Drawing on the perspectives in Chapter 4 and the information in Chapter 6, the following management priorities can be outlined:

- Investigation of the possibility of early retirement for Mrs Underwood who seems reluctant to contribute to the changes incumbent upon primary education in the 1990s. If a younger teacher on a lower scale point were appointed, as well as bringing in enthusiasm and commitment, there would be financial benefits. On Mrs Underwood's departure her A allowance could be reallocated.

- Mrs Elkins appears to be highly committed and may be a candidate for the language post or for co-ordinating pastoral care and parental links. On the other hand her existing commitments may be sufficiently onerous for the time being.

- There is an obvious need to appoint a Technology co-ordinator and to provide a general staff development programme in this area. Miss Ingram appears to have some skills and enthusiasm and would be a suitable candidate.

- A co-ordinator is required to monitor the development of National Curriculum History and Geography and to initiate staff and curriculum development in these areas.

- There should be rationalisation of the part-time teacher provision with the aim of amalgamating this into a more substantive post.

- The whole area of staff development and job descriptions for teaching and non-teaching staff needs urgent action. This is especially necessary so that every area of the curriculum can have a co-ordinator. Alongside this, governors and senior management must formulate a coherent allowance policy.

- It is necessary to consider extra provision of non-teaching assistants.

BUDGETARY REVIEW PART 3: PHYSICAL RESOURCES

Priorities should be established from the earlier review in Chapter 6. These should include specific items such as decoration, furnishings and occasional repairs rather than recurring minor maintenance.

Drawing on the perspectives in Chapter 4 and the information in Chapter 6, the following management priorities can be outlined:

- To improve the school's image an attractive and prominent school sign is needed.

- The entrance hall needs a major refurbishment to project a positive image and a welcoming environment to visitors and prospective parents.

- External work such as repairing the brick wall and providing playground markings would improve the external environment.

- Internal improvements such as office blinds and a programme of decoration are other priorities.

Current spending patterns and contract charges reveal that the cost of grounds maintenance this year is only £3,017 and a surplus of £2,122 is going to be available for virement.

BUDGETARY REVIEW PART 4: EXTERNAL RESOURCES

A statement should be made of desirable developments such as links to be built up with parents or industry, the potential for marketing and income generation and for improved access to LEA services.

Drawing on the perspectives in Chapter 4 and the information in Chapter 6, the following management priorities can be outlined:

- The school needs to develop a marketing strategy so that it can effectively manage its reputation in the community. There are several aspects of this, and it is important that they are not treated in isolation but are an integral part of the overall strategy. From the initial review it is clear that the school brochure must be given urgent attention and that the uniform may need reconsidering. The major area of home school relationships must be developed to incorporate curricular, social and fund-raising activities.

- There should be regeneration of interest in the PTA for social and fund-raising activities and to build stronger links between the parents and the school.

- Extra non-LEA financial provision could be secured by investigating a number of areas. Sponsorship and lettings are obvious examples as well as PTA-based events. The use of convenants is also an area worth consideration.

SUMMARY

The purpose of this first part of the three stages of budgeting has been to outline necessary developments in the areas of Curriculum, Staffing, Physical Resources and External Resources. Without this grouping of priorities it would be impossible to start the resource planning stage which seeks to predict the cost and revenue implications of decisions over the next three years.

The School Management Plan (Chapter 4) should not only highlight these necessary changes but should draw up a timetable for implementation that prioritises them. It is also necessary to appreciate the integrated nature of the changes in the four areas. An example of this is Technology which not only requires a new curriculum policy and new equipment and resources but also requires the appointment of a curriculum co-ordinator. This is also true for National Curriculum developments in History and Geography.

While this chapter has concentrated on proposing changes needed over the next three years the demands of managing the existing curriculum and other provision in the school also have to be considered. The annual or termly ordering of stock such as replacement books and materials will make its normal demands on the budgetary processes. The school will have to calculate carefully how much money allocated for capitation it should spend on normal stocks and replacement orders. There may then be some funds left over to meet the needs of the new developments but extra funding will also be required. It is here that the benefits of resource flexibility afforded by LMS become very apparent. The school will be able to look at the possibilities of virement in the budget to fund curriculum and other changes that could take place at a faster pace if reallocated funds were available. In the current year at the case study school the surplus of £2,122 on grounds maintenance provides a good example of this sort of possibility. In the longer term, staffing changes such as the retirement of Mrs Underwood would provide considerable scope for resource reallocations.

Having considered the proposed developments it is important to realise that not all change has a financial cost. Some changes require reorganisation of resources while others require a redesignation of responsibilities. For example, the appointment of curriculum co-ordinators in a number of areas will not result in extra expenditure, since all staff should expect to take on this sort of role.

This chapter has brought together the various reviews in order to highlight the developments necessary in the case study school. The reader, after consideration of the case study, may be able to suggest others. This critical stage provides a framework upon which planning can now take place. Having gone through this first of the three stages in the budgetary process it is hoped that the reader can apply the process to his or her school to assist in effective and efficient resource management.

The next chapter looks at the resource implications of these changes over the next three years, rather than just at the immediate costs, so that current decisions can be set in a medium term context.

8
Case Study Area Two: Budgetary Forecasting

In order to set immediate budgetary decisions in context it is necessary to highlight trends over the next three years to provide a medium term framework. To do this the school must produce an estimate of pupil numbers over these three years and this will largely determine the level of income from the LEA. An estimate must be made of the potential for generating income from other sources. It is also necessary to examine the nature and implications of any curriculum and other changes which the school plans to make so that the future budgetary expenditure position can be identified.

To undertake this forecasting exercise the school will need to produce the following:

- a forecast of the pupil roll over the next three years

- a prediction of the LMS income budget over these three years at current prices

- an outline of other potential sources of income

- an estimate of the resource implications of any proposed curriculum, staffing or physical resource changes over the next three years.

While this is going on a number of factors impact on the decision-making process in the case study school:

1. As predicted, the demands for new materials for the National Curriculum have resulted in the supplies and services element of the budget being overspent by about £1,000. Despite 'global warming' the second half of the Autumn Term is the coldest for many years and the long range weather forecast for Janaury and February is very bleak. This could lead to a £1,200 overspend on energy costs.

2. Planning permission has been granted for a new housing development on the edge of your catchment area for fifty new houses to be built during 1991/2.

3. A member of the governing body has been on a course about 'managing a school's reputation and marketing' and wishes to report back to the head and governing body about this.

BUDGETARY FORECAST PART 1: PUPIL ROLL

It would appear that the LEA's predictions do not take account of the recruitment potential of the new housing estate or the fact that the new head intends to enhance the school's image in the community. The school's own prediction of future roll would therefore be:

Age at 31/8	NC Yr Gp	Jan 1990 Actual	Jan 1991 Proj.	Jan 1992 Proj.	Jan 1993 Proj.	Jan 1994 Proj.
10	6	42	41	41	38	50
9	5	41	41	38	50	35
8	4	41	37	50	35	45
7	3	37	50	34	45	41
6	2	50	33	44	41	43
5	1	33	43	41	43	43
4	R	43	40	42	43	38
FTE		287	285	290	295	295

A realistic view would be to assume that it will not be feasible to improve upon the LEA estimates for January 1991. However, from then onwards it is very likely that the greatest improvement would be in the number of rising fives with some children in the older year groups moving into the district.

BUDGETARY FORECAST PART 2: INCOME PREDICTION

Chapter Four pointed out the importance when planning of being aware of future income trends. A school which has falling rolls has very different constraints to one which is expanding and therefore expecting to receive extra funding in future years.

Most of the factors which generate LEA income in the case study school will remain fairly constant over the next few years. However, the school believes that the pupil roll, which generates most of the income, will fluctuate in relation to the current year as follows:

1991	− 2
1991	+ 3
1993	+ 8
1994	+ 8

At present funding levels (£800-£840 per pupil depending on age) this will mean an income variation, compared with the current year, of approximately:

1991	− £1,600
1992	+ £2,400
1993	+ £6,400
1994	+ £6,400

In the long term, therefore, the school is looking at an expansion of resources although, in the interim, it may be difficult to deal with contraction. The management implication is that some projects may have to be introduced over a longer timescale than would have been desirable.

BUDGETARY FORECAST PART 3: OTHER SOURCES OF INCOME

As explained on page 30, there are various ways of supplementing the formula income from the LEA. It may be possible to seek funding from several 'official' sources such as government training initiatives, LEA advisers or the local council. Less formal income-generating activities could include letting the school premises and attracting funding from parents and industry. It is important to have whole school policies about such activities so that a clear procedure and set of criteria can be applied. There also needs to be a fairly clear picture of the hidden costs of some of the activities such as lettings and the use of the premises for PTA fundraising.

A three year prediction for Brentwich School might be as follows:

Other income	1992/2	1992/3	1993/4
Letting hall/ rooms	2 hrs per wk × 20 wks = £800	2 hrs per wk × 30 wks = £1,200	4 hrs per wk × 30 wks = £2,400
Letting grounds	2 hrs per wk × 20 wks = £200	4 hrs per wk × 20 wks = £400	6 hrs per wk × 20 wks = £600
PTA	£600	£1,200	£1,800
Sponsorship	£200	£300	£500
Covenants (parents and industry)	£660	£1,060	£1,600
TOTALS	£2,460	£4,160	£6,900

BUDGETARY FORECAST PART 4: THE RESOURCE IMPLICATIONS OF PROPOSED CHANGES

The Budgetary Review of Brentwich School in Chapter Seven highlighted many areas which needed some form of alteration or development. These vary in urgency and in terms of the implement-ation cost. Each will be considered here and an approximate cost will be given; in practice, a school would probably state the cost of various ways of achieving the desired outcome. This then provides the information which governors and senior managers need to have available later on when they are choosing between the alternatives.

At this stage, the areas of curriculum and staffing have been combined because they are very closely interconnected in terms of the need for resources. It has been assumed that the traditional capitation allowance is about £7,000 in this school.

Aims
In order to have a whole school approach to the **aims**, it will be necessary to set aside time for staff discussion. This could take place at staff meetings or on a training day.

The language curriculum
The major development of the **language** curriculum would require funding for books and materials as well as a considerable amount of staff development. Time would also be needed to develop links with parents so that they could reinforce the work at home and visit the school to give support. The funding for books and materials might be in the order of £500 in 1991, £500 in 1992 and £250 in 1993. If Mrs Underwood decided to opt for the LEA's early retirement scheme from August 31st 1991 there would be no cost to the school. She is paid on the top of Main Professional Grade (Jan 1991 cost £18,480 excluding A allowance) and, if the replacement was paid on Point 4 (Jan 1991 cost £12,127), savings would become available. If the A allowance were to be reallocated immediately, approximate savings would be calculated as follows:

Staff cost	1991/2		1992/3	1993/4
Mrs Underwood	5/12 salary	=£7,700	nil	nil
Replacement	7/12 salary	=£6,134	£12,464*	£13,120*
Total		£13,834	£12,464	£13,210
Saving compared with salary of Mrs Underwood (£18,480 without allowance)		£4,646	£6,016	£5,270

*allowing for increments.

Mrs Elkins could be asked to take responsibility for language. She would need guidance from senior management as well as time for attending training and for carrying out her role as co-ordinator in such a major area. A decision would need to be made about whether or not she should receive an allowance and, if so, the level, date and permanence of the appointment.

Technology
This also needs urgent attention because the National Curriculum should already be in place for some of the children. The first priority would be to appoint a co-ordinator who would then need time and resources to facilitate staff development and to help colleagues to

formulate a curriculum policy. At least £250 should be set aside in each of the next three years to fund equipment and materials. Some materials would have to be gathered from parents and local industry. The co-ordinator could consider the nature of any minor classroom improvements which would make practical work more effective and these could be funded out of the 'School Improvements' budget. The co-ordinator should also have the opportunity to visit other schools and centres and to attend courses in order to develop her/his own curriculum management expertise. It would appear that Miss Ingram could be asked to take on the co-ordinator's role.

History and Geography
Mrs Goddard could be asked to co-ordinate the introduction of National Curriculum **History and Geography** and to plan some investment in materials in 1991 (£175) and 1992 (£100). Further staff and curriculum development time would be needed, especially from April 1991 to the summer of 1992.

Special Needs
Rationalisation of the part-time staffing could create the opportunity for Mrs Allen to have a 0.9 **Special Needs** post at very little extra cost. She could then work more closely with her colleagues in preparing a policy for Special Needs, providing support and developing staff skills in dealing with any problems within the normal classroom environment. Here again a training day may prove valuable, possibly followed up by workshop sessions and intervisiting.

Music
If Mrs Underwood were to retire in August 1991, the school could appoint a teacher from September 1991 to co-ordinate **Music**. Development funding could be provided in April 1992 (£150) and 1993 (£100).

Maths
A decision needs to be taken quickly about the desirability of fully implementing the new **Maths** scheme for all age groups. This would cost approximately £1,000 in 1991, but if the present policy of gradual implementation was to be adhered to, the cost could be met annually from 'capitation'.

PSHE and RE

There needs to be clarification of responsibilities for co-ordinating **PSHE and RE**. There will be a time requirement so that the curriculum can be developed and this will result in a demand for materials. It is proposed to allocate £90 in 1992 and £110 in 1993.

Staff development

A review of policy regarding **staff development** and **roles and responsibilities** for both teaching and non-teaching staff could take place on a training day and then be continued through interviews with individuals and through work in groups. The needs of individuals and school would then be integrated. Although they are not compelled to do so, it is hoped that non-teaching staff would feel sufficiently involved to wish to take part in these activities.

Classroom assistant

It would be worth considering the employment (probably on a temporary contract) of a half-time **classroom assistant** in 1992 and 1993 when pupil rolls (and, hence, income) are expected to rise.

Premises

From the normal 'school improvements' budget a sum of £100 could be spent on a new **school sign**. The design of this may be an opportunity for links with the comprehensive school or with local industry.

Major inputs of funds and effort are needed to enhance the school's **entrance hall**. A phased programme would require £1,500 in 1991 and £250 in 1992. This should provide for redecoration, chairs, tables, display case, flexible screens and a noticeboard. Parents could be asked to supply plants and the children's work would provide an attractive display.

If it is given attention quite soon, the **brick wall** can be repaired out of the normal maintenance budget and, when it begins to generate resources, the PTA could be asked to fund the playground markings.

For effective working £300 should be spent on the **office blinds** in the coming financial year.

A rolling programme of **internal decoration** should be prepared, perhaps by a governor, and staff should be consulted about the details of the 'decor'. An average of £400 (at present prices) should be allocated and, hence, the programme would probably extend over seven to ten years.

Marketing

If there is to be an impact on pupil roll by January 1992, it is very important that a **marketing strategy** is developed in the near future and that all staff are involved. A training day should be devoted to this important area; perhaps an external consultant could be employed. It might be feasible to attract £200 sponsorship towards the cost of the new school brochure in 1991 and, therefore, another £200 would be needed. In future years, higher levels of sponsorship or advertising would be anticipated so that the brochure may become self-financing.

Parent governors could be asked to consider the whole area of **parental links** and PTA activities in order to involve a wider group of the school's partners.

SUMMARY

This chapter has highlighted the resource implications of the developments which seem to be required if Brentwich School is to meet the needs of children in the 1990s. In order to avoid confusion caused by excessive detail, many activities and issues have received scant attention here. It is, however, quite likely that the proposals will exceed the capacity of the budget and that a list of 'unfunded areas' will remain for consideration as time progresses. In addition, further, as yet unpredicted, demands will be placed on the funds in the short and medium term. This unpredictability means that a directional approach to planning is required in schools so that the plans are effectively flexible and responsive to change, yet have the general goals in view.

The first two stages of the budgetary process have now been described. The next chapter will show how these developments can be funded in the 1991/2 financial year.

9

Case Study Area Three: Budgetary Implementation

It is now early March and the school is creating the new budget for **implementation** in April 1991. The school needs to produce a detailed budget to present to the governors using the framework in Chapter 4 and, more specifically, the material from the first two budgetary stages as provided in Chapters 7 and 8.

The following additional information is available:

- The County Council, in trying to preserve the quality of education, increases its unit of resource funding level to equal the current level of inflation (10%).

- The pay award to all staff will be 10%.

The school will need to complete the budget for income and expenditure for 1991/92 and prepare a statement of the rationale for the decisions made.

In doing this it will be necessary to go through the following stages:

1. Calculate the sections of the income budget.
2. Calculate the sections of the expenditure budget.
3. Draw up a list of unfunded priorities for future action.

BUDGETARY IMPLEMENATION STAGE 1: INCOME CALCULATION

The pupil numbers at January 1991 (Form 7) are 285. When multiplied by the age weighting, this gives 293.45 age-weighted pupil units. Thus the first part of the income budget when multiplied by the unit of resource (increased by 10%) is as follows:

A. Aggregated Age Weighted Pupil Units × Unit of Resource
AWPU Current Year = 293.45 × £884.40 = £259,527

The next part of the income budget consists of three items: small school allowance, flat rate allowance and LMS allowance. The latter two remain constant while the former is adjusted to reflect the new pupil roll. The unit of resource has again been increased by 10%. This produces the following result.

B.	(1) Other Factors	
		Units
	Small school allowance	
	$360 - \text{NOR} = 75$	
	therefore $75 \times 0.12 =$	9.00
	Flat rate allowance	58.00
	LMS allowance	6.00
	Total units =	73.00
	73.00 units $\times$ £840.40	$= £61,349$

The premises section of the formula is calculated with the floor area and grounds area remaining constant and the unit of resource again being increased by 10%. The rates figure is funded at actual costs of £14,114. This produces the following result:

(2) Premises Formula	
(a) Floor area $\times$ funding per square metre	
$1523\text{m}^2 \times £5.247 = $	£ 7,991
(b) Grounds $\times$ funding per hect.	
1.49 hect $\times$ £4,168.84 =	£ 6,212
(c) Rates	£14,114 = £28,317

Special needs funding for the 1991/2 financial year is projected as follows:

(3) Special Needs formula	= £2,786

As a result of the over and underspendings which have been highlighted in earlier chapters, the out-turn from last year's budget is:

(4)	(i) Overspending:	Energy	£1,200
		Curriculum	
		Materials	£1,000
			£2,200
	(ii) Underspending:	Grounds	£2,122
		Supply	£2,100
			£4,222
	Surplus Balance C/F:		£2,022

The total income budget can thus be aggregated as follows:

INCOME BUDGET FOR 1991/92:

A. Aggregated Age Weighted Pupil Units × Unit of Resource
   AWPU Current Year = 293.45 × £884.40   = £259,527

B. (1) Other Factors

	Units
Small school allowance	
360 − NOR = 75	
therefore 75 × 0.12	9.00
Flat rate allowance	58.00
LMS allowance	6.00
Total units =	73.00
73.00 units × £840.40	=£ 61,349

(2) Premises Formula

(a) Floor area × funding per square metre
   $1523m^2$ × £5.247 =   £ 7,991

(b) Grounds × funding per hect.
   1.49 hect.   × £4,168.84 = £ 6,212

(c) Rates   £14,114

                                       =£ 28,317

(3) Special Needs Formula Funding   =£ 2,786

(4) C/F from previous year   =£ 2,022

Formula Budget Total   =**£354,001**

This represents the LEA funding for the school. Additional community based funds that are projected to be available are:

Letting hall/rooms 2 hrs per wk × 20 wks:	£	800
Letting grounds 2 hrs per wk × 20 wks:	£	200
PTA	£	600
Sponsorship	£	200
Covenants (parents & industry)	£	660
TOTAL	£2,460	

BUDGETARY IMPLEMENTATION STAGE 2: EXPENDITURE CALCULATION

It is proposed to deal with the expenditure budget in its three sections of Staffing, Premises and General Expenses.

The calculation of the first of these areas, that of Staffing, is based on a number of factors.

- Teacher staffing has been adjusted by Mrs Underwood taking early retirement on 31 August 1991 and being replaced by a teacher to co-ordinate Music on Point 4 of the Main Professional Grade. The Scale A allowance will not be reallocated in the remaining two terms of the financial year.

- Temporary contracts for Mrs Black and Mrs Carter are not renewed and their service terminates on 31 August 1991.

- Mrs Allen is to have an increased contract taking her to 0.9 of a full time post.

- Salary levels for staff have been adjusted to take account of the 10% pay rise on 1 April 1991 and incremental increases due on September 1 1991.

- Admin and support staff, midday supervision, caretaking and duty meals remain the same and costs are increased by 10%.

- The supply allocation in the previous year proved an excessive amount. In the 1991/2 financial year the school decides to join a supply insurance scheme offered by Ellison Teacher Insurance

Services Ltd. The current 'loss leader' price of this is £112 per teacher. The total cost in the first year will be £1,440. However, it is unlikely that the rates will remain so competitive in future years, so the decision is for one year only.

This produces the first part of the expenditure budget dealing with staffing as:

Staffing	
Teaching Staff	£257,834
Admin & Support Staff	£ 21,586
Midday Supervision	£ 6,118
Caretaking	£ 12,222
Supply	£ 1,440
Duty Meals	£ 1,650
	£300,850

The Premises part of the expenditure budget has been assessed as follows:

- Building Maintenance has been increased by 10% and a further £500 for the first phase of the redecoration programme giving a total of £6,734.

- Energy has been increased to £9,250 on the assumption that the winter will not be so severe.

- Rates are fixed at £14,114.

- Grounds Maintenance was overestimated and money was vired to other areas. The realistic assumption for this year is £3,319.

- The 'other premises' costs are estimated as £2,541.

The second part of the budget is thus:

Premises	
Building Maintenance	£ 6,734
Energy	£ 9,250
Rates (fixed amount)	£14,114
Grounds Maintenance	£ 3,319
Other Premises (Water rates, sewerage etc)	£ 2,541
	£35,958

In the General Expenses part of the budget the following allocations have been made:

- Supplies and Services have been increased by 10% for normal increases to £13,816 and then increased by £500 to fund the improvements to the Language scheme, £250 to implement further developments in the Technology scheme and £175 for National Curriculum History and Geography totalling £14,741.

- The planned school improvements are the office blinds at £300 and £375 for classroom improvements for practical areas, totalling £675.

- Advertising for one post this year is estimated at £400.

- The Marketing budget contributes £377 towards the cost of a school brochure and other expenses.

- The contingency fund remains at £1,000 for the time being.

This leaves the final section of the budget as:

Supplies & Services	£14,741
School Improvements	£ 675
Advertising	£ 400
Marketing	£ 377
Contingency	£ 1,000
	£17,193

The recommended expenditure budget for 1991/2 is therefore as follows:

Expenditure budget for 1991/2

Staff	£	£
Teaching Staff	257,834	
Admin & Support Staff	21,586	
Midday Supervision	6,118	
Caretaking	12,222	
Supply	1,440	
Duty Meals	1,650	
		300,850
Premises		
Building Maintenance	6,734	
Energy	9,250	
Rates (Fixed Amount)	14,114	
Grounds Maintenance	3,319	
Other Premises (Water rates, sewerage etc)	2,541	
		35,958
Other Services		
Supplies & Services	14,741	
School Improvements	675	
Advertising	400	
Marketing	377	
Contingency	1,000	
		17,193
Planned Expenditure Total		354,001

BUDGETARY IMPLEMENTATION STAGE 3 – FURTHER FUNDING PRIORITIES

The school has a number of areas which it has been unable to fund out of the current year's LEA budget. These are:

- £1,500 to refurbish the entrance hall.

- £1,000 to fully implement the new Maths scheme for all age groups immediately rather than the longer phased approach.

- £600 for playground markings and new playground apparatus.

- £123 extra for the marketing budget.

- £1,200 for an 'A' allowance to be allocated when the job description and staff development review is completed.

On page 92 a list of non-LEA sources of funding was given which totalled £2,460 of potential income. As and when this funding becomes available it can be allocated to some of the items on the above list. This will still leave some areas which cannot be funded at the present time. These will either have to wait for potential virement opportunities later in the year or form part of next year's budget.

Qualitative Changes
The changes described so far in this chapter have had a direct financial cost but other developments which have a time and commitment cost will also need to be activated during the year. These are listed below:

- Job descriptions are required and one outcome of this would be co-ordinators for all curricular areas.

- A staff development policy needs to be agreed and articulated.

- Training provision which will arise from the staff development policy will probably focus in the first instance on Language, Technology, History and Geography, Special Needs.

- A reformulation of the whole school aims is required.

- There should be a review of parental links for supporting curricular work and other home school relationships via a revived PTA.

- A major marketing effort is needed in the Summer Term 1991 using training days to develop a marketing strategy.

CONCLUSION

This chapter has established the budget for 1991/92. Building on the **review** and **forecasting** stages it has demonstrated the successful **implementation** of a balanced budget. It is important that the reader views this as a three stage process and not a simple accounting activity. It is also important that a positive view of resource management is established. While the school suffered a minor reduction in roll for the 1991/92 year it has managed to reorganise its resources and raise extra funding to provide a sound financial framework to facilitate effective educational provision for the 1991/92 year. By prioritising its marketing and relationships with its clients it is projecting forward for a marginally increasing roll and the financial benefits which that will bring.

Chapter 4 emphasised the importance of **evaluation**: this will highlight resource use which has been effective and will also identify areas where alternative strategies are required. For example, in the case study school it would be desirable to evaluate the success of the marketing strategy and of the staff development activities in the language area. The form of evaluation should be clear from the start. It is unwise to attempt to evaluate too many activities in a fairly small school because the outcome will be superficial and of little value.

We hope that readers can apply the principles established in Chapters 7, 8 and 9 in order to provide an effective resource management framework in their own schools.

10
Key Implications for Primary School Management

This book has been arranged in three main sections. The first considered the nature and dimensions of LMS and of income and expenditure in the primary school. The second section discussed the importance of school development planning and the role of the people involved while the final section introduced a case study school and implemented a four-stage budgetary process.

It is useful to summarise the key management points which have arisen.

1. An appreciation of the fundamental change in the nature of the relationship between schools, LEAs and central government and that LMS consists of five interconnected factors which have a dynamic effect on schools. These factors are:

   - delegated finance
   - formula funding
   - open enrolment
   - staffing delegation
   - performance indicators

2. A clear understanding of the structure of income and expenditure patterns in primary schools and the scope that schools have to utilise them in a decentralised and creative way for the benefit of children's education.

3. The central and fundamental importance of a School Management Development Plan which sets resource management in the context of the whole school. This is essential if finance is to be seen as a facilitator of the educational process.

4. A focus on how a process is managed as well as on the process itself as a key to successful resource management. Schools need to establish and clarify effective working relationships between the various partners in the school management process *before* they

grapple with the technicalities of LMS. This means considering such key issues as:

- decision-making structures that are clear and defined;

- appropriate dissemination of information, effective consultation and participation;

- prioritising and effective time management;

- the need for training and skill development for the partners in the school to take on the new roles and responsibilities.

5. A management approach to budgeting that moves away from the purely administrative and functional purposes of book-keeping to one which sees the fundamental stages in a *strategic* approach to budgeting. These are:

- **Budgetary Review** – which establishes the current position of the schools.

- **Budgetary Forecasting** – which sets financial decisions within a medium term context.

- **Budgetary Implementation** – which brings together plans and priorities and gives financial reality to educational plans.

- **Budgetary Evaluation** – which highlights the effectiveness of resource use in meeting educational needs.

Appendix: An LEA Approach to LMS

SURREY'S APPROACH TO THE LOCAL MANAGEMENT OF SCHOOLS by PETER LEVELL

PLANNING THE SCHEME
Surrey's Scheme of Local Management was approved by the Authority and submitted to the Secretary of State in July 1989, and exactly two months later approval was received from the Secretary of State to Surrey's submission with a few minor amendments. Surrey's was the second scheme in the country to be approved, along with Suffolk and after Norfolk.

Pilot scheme experience
In developing the Scheme to comply with Government requirements, we were able to build on substantial experience of partial local management in our secondary schools. A pilot scheme was started in 1985, extended in 1987 (with one school and one sixth form college piloting a 'total budget' approach), and, following a full evaluation, offered to all secondary schools in Surrey in 1988. Within a year all of them had voluntarily opted to join the scheme. The Surrey Local Financial Management Scheme delegated about 10% of a school's budget to Governing Bodies (75% in the case of the 'total budget' schools), as compared with about 4% for traditional capitation allowance and some 70% to 75% under the Government's scheme. The strength of Surrey's approach to local management has been the participatory style of management. A working group of Headteachers was established to work with the Authority in 1984 and develop the early scheme. This group has met at least once per term since that time and a group representing the Teacher Associations and NALGO was also established early on. The participation of the Teacher Associations in the evaluation of the pilot scheme was invaluable and their support for its extension to other Surrey secondary schools was a significant help in securing widespread support for Surrey's approach.

Commitment to improving quality through local management
There has been strong support in Surrey both politically and professionally for the philosophy and principles of local management. This strength derives from the conviction that local management is not an end in itself, but a means to an end, namely the improvement of the quality of education and the opportunities afforded to pupils and students in our schools and colleges through delegating the management of cash resources, personnel and premises to local level. From the outset of Surrey's pilot scheme, the tangible educational benefits to pupils of the flexibility offered through local management have been evaluated, whether in terms of additional facilities in the classroom, providing extra opportunities for professional development for teachers, additional responsibility posts to retain qualified and experienced staff, or adaptations to buildings to improve the learning environment.

In developing Surrey's scheme to comply with the requirements of the Education Reform Act 1988, that same conviction has underpinned the whole approach. The foreword to Surrey's scheme states that "Surrey LEA is firmly committed to the philosophy and principles of local management, and to the over-riding aim that the management opportunities afforded to Governing Bodies and Headteachers should lead to improved quality of education and learning for the pupils in our schools and colleges." The Surrey approach has been to emphasise the primacy of the curriculum and of improving the quality of the education and learning offered to pupils. We have seen local management as being one of the ways in which that can be effectively secured.

Direction through a Reform Steering Group
In June 1988 a Reform Steering Group was established comprising senior officers and inspectors, together with the Deputy County Treasurer and the Vice-Principal of the 'total budget' Sixth Form College seconded half-time, to oversee the co-ordination and implementation of the Education Reform Act and in particular to prepare and develop a Scheme of Local Management. Before the end of July some twenty working groups had been set up to undertake the work needed on various aspects of the Scheme of Local Management. Some of these were confined to the Education Department, but the majority were corporate working groups – in total some fifty officers (about half in the Education Department) were members of these working groups and contributed to a greater or lesser extent in

developing the Scheme. These groups examined in depth matters such as training for staff and Governors, the development of performance indicators, special needs, arrangements for adult education and community use, the development of a resource allocation formula, management information systems, matters related to property and personnel, finance and legal issues.

Extensive consultation
In addition to the group of Secondary Heads already referred to, a group of twelve Primary Heads was established for consultation, and these Heads' Consultative Groups met frequently during the latter part of 1988. There was also a series of consultations with the Teacher Associations, Trade Union and Diocesan Authorities. All these groups were actively involved in commenting on initial draft papers as the Scheme was prepared. The Draft Scheme was approved as a basis for formal consultation with Governing Bodies and other groups in December 1988 and that consultation took place in the spring term 1989. A series of briefing meetings was held for Governors in January 1989 throughout the County and Head-teachers were kept informed of progress through meetings and correspondence. There were several seminars for County Councillors and Senior Officers of all Departments. A number of revisions were made in the light of the comments and responses of those who were consulted, and the formula was further developed to comply with the requirements of the Department of Education and Science. One of the strengths of Surrey's approach was to invest heavily in the time needed for effective communication and consultation, and the outcome of this participatory approach has been that the Scheme has secured widespread understanding and acceptance throughout the County.

A phased programme, with a "dry-run"
Building on to the experience in the secondary sector with a limited local financial management scheme, we have also operated a 'dry-run' of as much as possible of the Government's scheme in five primary and five secondary schools from April 1989. This experience has proved extremely useful in testing out training programmes and materials, management information systems, the development of performance indicators and the amount and responsibility level of administrative staff time which may be necessary for schools to undertake local management.

Surrey's timetable for implementing local management is:

April 1990 –   all 59 secondary schools and 44 primary schools;

April 1991 –   186 primary schools, including all those with
               more than 200 on roll;

April 1992 –   all remaining 144 primary schools.

Until Governing Bodies take on their local management responsibilities, the Authority must manage formula-based budgets for
schools with delegation. This is a completely new task facing local
authorities, and in Surrey we have reorganised parts of the four Area
Education Offices and established Local Management Units with
staff to manage the individual budgets of schools until the Governors
take over this responsibility under the Local Management Scheme.
So that these budgets can be managed effectively the Education
Committee have formally delegated to the CEO powers of virement
across all budget heads for these schools, and powers to determine
the numbers and grades of school staff. Since April 1990, 330
primary schools are being managed by the Authority in this way.
    One of the early tasks was to identify all the items of expenditure
which fall in various County budgets and which relate to expenditure
on primary and secondary schools, so that they could be brought
together to form the 'general schools budget'. From this the
mandatory and discretionary exceptions are deducted and the
remaining 'aggregated schools budget' is distributed to individual
schools on the basis of a formula. Many of the mandatory and
discretionary exceptions identified by Authorities are for similar
categories of expenditure and in Surrey they total about 29% of the
general schools budget. The balance, the aggregated schools budget
to be distributed on the basis of a formula, totals some £150m.

DEVELOPING THE RESOURCE ALLOCATION FORMULA

It is the development of the formula which has proved one of the
most difficult tasks facing Authorities in producing their schemes of
local management. In a County such as Surrey, with both urban and
rural areas, sixth form colleges, large and small secondary schools
and primary schools ranging from small village schools with less
than 30 on roll to large middle schools, this was a daunting task. The
formula had to be 'simple, clear and predictable', allocate 75% on

the basis of age-weighted pupil numbers, and relate to schools' 'objective needs', not historic expenditure.

A main formula and four sub-formulae
The approach in Surrey was to have a main formula to deliver resources for teaching staff, support staff, language assistants, caretakers, midday supervision, advertising and recruitment, supplies and services, teachers' travel, support for small schools and clerking of Governing Bodies. This was on the basis that all these items would relate to the size of schools, based on age-weighted pupil numbers for the most part. It was thought that there were certain items of expenditure where the needs of different age groups would be different from the weightings in the main formula. Four sub-formulae were therefore developed for supply cover, examination fees, premises and special needs.

The main formula and the objective needs of schools
It was extremely important that the main formula should be as accurate as possible in meeting the needs of schools, since this formula delivers 86% of the aggregated schools budget. The approach adopted was to identify the cash value of County policies rather than examining historic expenditure. Initially one of the four Areas of the County was taken and the cash value of County policies for all schools in this Area was identified, covering all the items of expenditure to be included within the main formula. In particular, the 'target'/pupil/teacher ratio was taken as the measure of County policy for the provision of teaching staff, together with additional teachers for curriculum support in smaller schools, incentive allowances at the projected 1990 level and Heads' and Deputy Heads' salaries in accordance with the (Burnham) grouping of each school. All of this information was put into a Lotus 1-2-3 spreadsheet and weightings were established for the different age groups and adjusted so that the formula would deliver the closest fit possible to the cash value of County policies. As well as the age-weighted pupil number element in the main formula, there were two further components − a subsidy to small schools and colleges to provide curriculum support, and a flat rate allocation of pupil units in order to assist with meeting the basic costs inherent, for example, in staffing establishments, with every school having a Headteacher, and a basic provision of clerical, administrative and caretaking staff.
Eventually the cash value of County policies was put into the

Lotus spreadsheet for all 439 schools in Surrey and the formula, by a process of iteration, was refined to produce the closest fit of the weightings within its various components to the cash value of County policies.

The age-weighted pupil numbers component of the main formula delivers 84% of the resources of the main formula; the flat rate allocation of pupil units (see table 1) delivers 14% of the resources of the main formula; the small school subsidy delivers 2%. This is a tapering subsidy, providing smaller schools with an additional fraction of a pupil unit on the extent to which its numbers on roll fall below a boundary point (see table 2). It is also worth mentioning that Surrey will be assisting small schools with meeting the actual costs of salaries where these exceed average costs.

Table 1: A flat rate allocation
Each school receives an allocation of pupil units irrespective of current enrolment, related to its age band. The rate is:

Type of School	*Flat Rate Allocation of Pupil Units*	
First (4-8)	45	*Plus* 6 more
Junior (8-11)	49	units for local
Middle (8-12)	49	management primary
Primary (4-11)	58	schools to provide
Combined First and Middle (4-12)	58	resources for extra
		administrative staff.
Secondary 11/12-16	110	
Secondary 11/12-19	118	
Sixth Form College	128	

Table 2: A subsidy to small schools and colleges
This subsidy operates in each age-band (other than Nursery) to provide curriculum support. Below a boundary point of numbers on roll (regarded as a minimum size for viability without subsidy) the school receives an additional fraction of a pupil unit on the extent to which its numbers on roll fall below the boundary. The subsidy is per pupil below the boundary point as follows:

Type of School	Boundary Point	Additional Weighting
First (4-8)	120	0.12
Junior (8-11)	180	0.12
Middle (8-12)	240	0.12
Primary (4-11)	300	0.12
Combined First and Middle (4-12)	360	0.12
Secondary (11/12-16)	720	0.37
Secondary (11/12-19)	870	0.37
Sixth Form College	500	0.37

The principles of the main formula can be represented graphically:

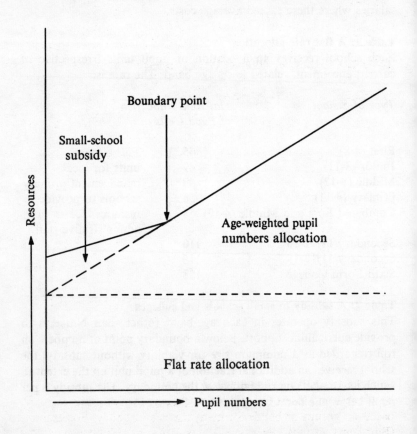

After some fifty or more iterations an optimum fit was obtained with almost 77% of schools having a variation from the cash value of County policies of less than plus or minus 2% (see tables 3 and 4).

Table 3: Comparison of Main Formula with the cash value of County policies

% Difference	Number of Schools	No as % of total
0%-1%	229	52.2%
1%-2%	108	24.6%
2%-3%	27	6.2%
3%-5%	33	7.5%
5% +	42	9.6%
Totals	439	100%

Table 4: Variation for different types of school

% Difference	First	Middle	Combined	Secondary 12/16	Secondary 12/19	VI Form Colleges	Total
−10		1					1
−5		1			1		2
−4					3		3
−3	1		2	1	4		8
−2	4	2	1		4		11
−1	46	17	10	5	2	2	82
	63	24	7	7	5	2	108
+1	41	59	10	3	6	2	121
+2	11	1	7	1	5	1	26
+3	2		11	2	1		16
+4	3		6	1			10
+5	7		3	2			12
+10	30		2				32
	6			1			7
Totals	214	105	59	23	31	7	439

Some variation is inevitable with a formula approach and there will be winners and losers because the resourcing for schools is currently based on groups or bands for many aspects of policy. For example (Burnham) groups determine the salaries of Headteachers and Deputies and the number of incentive allowances. There is therefore a stepped or banded approach for much funding of schools at present, whereas a formula based mainly on pupil numbers is a linear approach. This can be represented diagrammatically as follows:

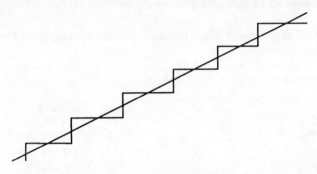

The 'staircase' represents how schools are funded at present for many aspects of their expenditure, whereas the ladder represents a formula based approach. Put another way, the difference of one pupil can currently cause a school to jump up or down one school group with all that implies in terms of funding, whereas under a formula system the difference of one pupil will mean a small addition or reduction to a school's budget.

The four sub-formulae
For the supply cover formula, the weightings were determined on the basis of a greater need for supply cover at primary level because of the higher class contact ratio and less need for supply cover for pupils aged 16+. The weightings for the examination fees formula for the age groups 15-18 were based on a study of examination entries at all secondary schools and colleges, including a comparison of access factors related to the relevant age groups and the costs of examinations at different levels. The premises formula provides for an allocation based on actual cost levels for general rates and for rent for buildings and playing fields provided to meet basic statutory school requirements, an allocation for grounds based on the County entitlement of playing field area, an allocation for swimming pool maintenance based on an equal share for each pool, and a condition factor allocation for internal redecoration based on the remaining three years of a seven year county programme, with the major part of the resources for premises (mainly energy and building maintenance) then being allocated on the basis of 40% related to numbers on roll and 60% related to the total cleaning area of the school buildings.

The special needs formula provides assistance for non-statemented special needs pupils using the results of the County's screening procedures at ages 7 and 11. The expected numbers of children with special educational needs (reading quotient less than 85) will be calculated based on County averages for the total numbers on roll. This figure is compared with the actual number of children with special educational needs and the higher of the two figures used to calculate the additional support for a school. A second component in the special needs formula will provide a school with additional resources for the incidence of social deprivation based on the number of pupils identified as eligible to receive free school meals as a proportion of the total number in the County.

Aggregation of pupil-related factors

All the directly pupil related factors in the main formula, the supply cover formula, the examination fees formula and the pupil number element in the premises formula, have been aggregated to produce the age weightings (rounded to two decimal points) which will deliver almost 77% of the aggregated schools budget (see table 5).

Table 5: Aggregated pupil age weightings

September Age	3	4	5	6	7	8	9	10	11
Weighting	1.00	1.00	1.00	1.00	1.00	1.05	1.05	1.05	1.05

September Age	12	13	14	15	16	17	18
Weighting	1.50	1.50	1.50	1.62	2.24	2.24	2.21

We have deliberately avoided putting cash figures into any part of the formula, preferring to use statistics such as pupil numbers and floor area. The cash value of each pupil unit will be established on an annual basis – currently the aggregated unit of resource is £775.75 for each pupil unit, and the main formula unit of resource (for Tables 1 and 2) is £709.19.

Analysis of Aggregated Schools Budget

An analysis has been made of the proportions of the aggregated schools budget which are distributed by the different elements in the formula and by age-weighted numbers on roll (see table 6).

Table 6: Analysis of Aggregated Schools Budget

	% distributed by age-weighted numbers on roll	% distributed by other factors	% Totals
Main Formula			
Age-weighted pupil nunbers	72.18		
Extra for nursery class pupils		0.30	
Small School Subsidy		1.76	
Flat Rate Allocation		11.81	
Sub-total	72.18	13.87	86.05
Supply Cover	1.85		1.85
Exam Fees	0.90		0.90
Premises			
Delegated Maintenance (24.6% of total maintenance)	0.69	1.04	
Energy	0.92	1.37	
Water rates and sewerage	0.20	0.29	
Rates		3.52	
Rents		0.04	
Swimming Pools		0.08	
Grounds		1.21	
Sub-total	1.81	7.55	9.36
Special Needs		1.34	
Small Schools variations in teaching costs		0.50	
Totals	76.74	23.26	100.00

Comparison with historic costs

The full working of the formula has been compared with the current actual expenditure of each school in Surrey and there are of course very much wider variations than the comparison of the main formula with the cash value of County policies shown. This is to be expected because there are many schools whose expenditure is not what a strict application of County policy would provide. For example, there are some secondary schools which, because of falling rolls, have more teachers than the target pupil/teacher ratio would give them. There are other schools, particularly in the primary sector, which have fewer teachers than the target pupil/teacher ratio would provide, because the total number of teachers in Surrey is currently controlled by the overall application of target pupil/teacher ratios. This maldistribution of resources will be rectified over the transitional period of four years, since the formula based budgets will in effect transfer some resources from the secondary sector to the primary sector and achieve a closer adherence to County policy than has been achieved in the past. It is in this sense that the formula is related to objective needs and does not continue historic patterns of expenditure. It is recognised that the formula does continue existing policies, but the formula is flexible, and the weightings for particular age-groups can easily be adjusted to deliver resources for policy changes which may be approved. If, for example, additional resources were to be provided to assist primary schools with the introduction of the national curriculum, the general schools budget would be increased, and the weightings for primary pupils adjusted so that the extra resources would be delivered to primary schools.

PREPARING FOR IMPLEMENTATION

To plan a Scheme is one thing, to implement it another. During 1989 we were making vigorous preparations for implementing local management in 1990.

Management Information Systems
One major aspect of this is the development of appropriate management information systems, and a team of officers, together with external consultants, have been designing software and testing out hardware. The timetable for this is extremely tight and leaves barely sufficient time for testing the software before it will have to be installed in schools.

Training
Another major task is training of staff and Governors. We have appointed a Head of Local Management Training and a Governors Training Co-ordinator, both formerly Secondary Heads, and various other staff are involved in developing the training programmes. Training has already started in management awareness and management skills, and dates have been fixed for training in personnel, financial procedures and information systems. In total every school in

the first phase received seven days' training before local management was implemented in April 1990. The logistics of organising and delivering training for Heads, senior staff and administrative staff both in schools and Area Offices has proved to be a challenging task, as has the training of some of the 6,000 Governors there are in Surrey.

Extra staffing support in schools

The Education Committee have approved additional resources for Administrative staff in schools as they undertake local management, an average of 12 hours for Primary Schools, and a Senior Officer grade post for Secondary Schools. These resources will be available to schools from the January prior to the April concerned so that staff appointed can attend the training courses and be involved in the preparation of budgets and management plans.

Support services from the Authority

The structure of the Education Department and its Area Offices is being reviewed and reorganised to meet the changing role which local authorities will have. Fewer staff will be involved in administrative tasks and the priority will be to provide a high quality support service for schools, particularly from the Inspectorate and from Area-based personnel, finance and information systems staff.

Manuals for schools

All schools in Surrey have already been provided with a copy of the Local Management of Schools Initiative *Practical Guide* which is proving extremely helpful. Good use is being made of training materials produced by the LMS Initiative and every school has recently been sent a copy of Brent Davies' and Chris Braund's book entitled *Local management of Schools – An Introduction for Teachers, Governors and Parents*. We are also producing our own manuals of guidance on personnel, premises, financial procedures and information systems. As well as providing this guidance, we are working on model personnel procedures, such as disciplinary procedures, grievance procedures etc. The objective is to agree such documents with the Teacher Associations and Trade Unions and seek the approval of the Education Committee so that there is one common procedure for all staff (teaching and non-teaching) in schools and in colleges, hopefully including further education colleges. These procedures will then be commended to Governing Bodies who will be able to adopt them if they so wish as their own procedures. Negotiations on the first of these, the disciplinary procedure, are almost complete and a procedure with such widespread support and agreement will be a significant achievement and of great assistance to Governing Bodies as they undertake their local management responsibilities.

Performance Indicators

A good deal of work has also been done in developing performance indicators for schools with substantial help from the Audit Commission. A statistical profile has been developed which will give basic information about each school, such as the numbers on roll, the occupancy rate, the number of teaching staff, the pupil/teacher ratios, the teacher contact ratios, class sizes, the amount of time spent on the core and foundation subjects in the national curriculum and on other subjects, national assessment results and examination results. The profile will also include financial information and certain cost indicators such as the cost of energy and repairs per square metre. Many of these figures will be compared with Surrey averages and with national averages where appropriate and where possible. While these profiles are not intended to describe everything that is happening in a school and they are limited to what is 'measurable', they will nevertheless be of significant help both to Governors and to the Authority in assessing the effectiveness of schools and their achievements.

Whole school management development plans.

Finally, one of the most important things that we are doing is working on a framework for a whole school management development plan to assist schools in their own forward planning. This is being developed jointly with the Inspectorate and will encourage schools to focus on identifying their objectives for the curriculum and the character of the school over a period of four or five years, assessing where they are now, and in the light of the resources and opportunities made available through local management, establishing their priorities including in-service training needs, and drawing up their management plan. The framework being developed will assist schools in this process, will focus primarily on the curriculum and the school's educational objectives and ensure that a positive view is taken of local management as a means for achieving the educational objectives of the school.

Glossary

Academic year. This runs from September until August.

Advisory teachers are employed by the LEA to use their curriculum expertise and knowledge to train and develop other teachers in schools.

Audit Commission. An organisation which examines the efficiency of local government services.

AWPU. Age Weighted Pupil Units. A figure arrived at through multiplying the number of children by a weighting for age.

Capital expenditure refers to money set aside for major new building or other long term expenditure programmes.

Capitation is the term given to the budgets that schools have received in the past, based on pupils' age and numbers, from which they have bought books and educational equipment.

Competitive tendering. Under this system a number of firms or companies are asked to put in bids for work to be done. The school can choose the quote best suited to its budget and requirements.

Contingency fund. A sum of money put to one side for unforeseen or unquantifiable future expenditure.

DION. Diagnosis of Individual and Organisation Needs. An instrument used for school review.

Financial year. This runs from April 1st until March 31st.

Formula. The means by which LEAs will share out the money available for delegated school budgets.

GRIDS. Guidelines for Internal Development in Schools. A process of institutional review.

Historical budgeting is the practice of basing one year's budget on what had been received in previous years.

Incentive allowances are usually paid to teachers who take on additional responsibilities, such as curriculum leadership roles, in schools.

Incremental budgets are associated with historical costs and are the annual adjustments made to the figures to allow for minor adjustments but the budget remains approximately the same.

Incremental scales. These are the points on the pay scales that teachers progress through on an annual basis up to a maximum point.

Open enrolment is where parents can choose to which school they send their children.

Statemented children are those who have been referred to the LEA's educational psychologists who have considered the child's problems serious enough to merit their being kept under annual review. These reports are the child's statements.

Supply teachers are extra staff brought in to cover for sick or absent teachers.

Support Staff. A term used to refer to non-teaching staff in schools.

Virement. The transfer of money from one expenditure heading to another.

Further Reading

Caldwell, B.J. & Spinks, J.M., *The Self-Managing School* (Falmer Press 1988).

Coopers & Lybrand Associates, *Local Management of Schools: A Report to the Department of Education and Science* (HMSO 1988).

Davies, B., 'The Key Issues of Financial Delegation', *Education* Vol 170 No 18 (30th October 1987).

Davies, B., 'Three Steps to Lift-Off: Unfolding an LFM Training Strategy in Leicestershire', *Education* Vol 172 No 6 (5th August 1988).

Davies, B., & Braund, C., *Local Management of Schools – An Introduction for Teachers, Governors and Parents* (Northcote House, 1989).

Davies, B., Ellison, L., Osborne, A., & West-Burnham, J., *Education Management for the 1990s* (Longman 1990).

Downes, P., *Local Financial Management in Schools* (Blackwell 1988).

Hill, D., Oakley-Smith, B., Spinks, J., *Local Management of Schools* (Paul Chapman Publishing, 1990).

Knight, B. *Managing School Finance* (Heinemann 1983).

Messer, J., *LMS in Action* (Macmillan, 1990).

Thomas, H., 'Pupils as Vouchers', *Times Educational Supplement* (2nd December 1988).

Thomas, H., *Local Management of Schools in Action* (Cassell 1989).

Useful Addresses

Assistant Masters and Mistresses Association, 7 Northumberland Street, London WC2N 5DA.

Audit Commission, 157-159 Buckingham Palace Road, London SW1W 9SP.

Campaign for the Advancement of State Education, President Joan Sallis, 49 Lauderdale Drive, Petersham, Richmond, Surrey.

Centre for Education Management, Bronte Hall, Leeds Polytechnic, Beckett Park, Leeds LS6 3QS.

Chartered Institute of Public Finance and Accountancy, 3 Robert Street, London WC2N 6BH.

Department of Education and Science, Elizabeth House, York Road, London SE1 7PH.

National Association of Head Teachers, Holly House, 6 Paddockhall Rd, Haywards Heath, West Sussex RH16 1RG.

National Association of Governors and Managers, 81 Rustlings Road, Sheffield S11 7B.

National Association of School Masters/Union of Women Teachers, Hillscourt Education Centre, Rose Hill, Rednal, Birmingham B45 8RS.

National Confederation of Parent Teacher Associations, 43 Stonebridge Road, Northfleet, Gravesend, Kent DA11 9DS.

National Union of Teachers, Hamilton House, Mabledon Place, London WC1H 9BD.

Society of Education Officers, 21-27 Lambs Conduit St, London WC1N 3NJ.

Secondary Headteachers Association, Chancery House, 107 St Paul's Road, London N1 2NB.

Index

More books on
Education Management

The following pages contain details of a selection of other titles on Education Management. For further information, and details of our Inspection Copy Service, please apply to:

Northcote House Publishers Ltd, Plymbridge House, Estover Road, Plymouth PL6 7PZ, United Kingdom. Tel: Plymouth (0752) 705251. Fax: (0752) 777603. Telex: 45635.

A selection of catalogues and brochures is usually available on request.

Local Management of Schools
Brent Davies & Chris Braund

Written by two consultants in this important field, this book meets the pressing need for an introductory handbook to help governors, teachers and parents get to grips with major new responsibilities now becoming mandatory. Readable and practical, the book spells out the new legislation and what it means, the new financial structure in secondary and primary schools, the new role of Head teachers and governors in delegated school management, and what it means for the future. Complete with case studies and suggested management exercises.

'The nine main chapters, each dealing with a different aspect, are easy to read, comparatively jargon-free, and gave me a very good overview of LMS.... This reference book will justify a place in any educational establishment because of its accessible information and advice.' *Junior Education*. 'Well favoured by the brevity/practicality formula, written with governors and parents in mind as well as teachers. It is strong on illustrative yet simple graphics and tables and does not shirk the consequences of falling numbers.' *Times Educational Supplement*

Paperback, 96 pages, tables.

Marketing the Primary School
Brian Hardie

Schools have always had an eye on their 'reputation' and standing within the local community. However, open enrolment and competition for pupil numbers following the 1988 Education Reform Act have put a much greater value on the relationship which schools need to have with both parents and pupils. Now, in order to increase — and even maintain — pupil numbers, schools will be under much greater pressure to market themselves effectively. The author, who has been running courses in marketing and reputation management for primary school heads, shows how the primary school can be successfully promoted, stretching precious resources to make the most of contacts with the local community. Contents: Preface, the school in its marketplace, reputation management, marketing the school, meeting the customer, the prospectus and other communications, handling the media, further reading, useful addresses, glossary, index.

Brian Hardie MA DLC is a Senior Lecturer in Education Management at Crewe & Alsager College, and runs courses in marketing and reputation management for primary school Heads.

Paperback, 144 pages, illustrated.

The School Development Plan
From Draft to Action
Chris Braund

The Education Reform Act 1988 will soon require each of the 28,000 state primary and secondary schools in Britain to draw up and put into action their own School Development Plan. In this document they must define the human, financial and physical resources available to them, and show how these resources will be used to attain specified goals within a specified timescale. Written by a specialist at the forefront of education management *School Development Plans* will be welcomed as an urgently needed step-by-step manual to help every head teacher and governor understand and master this new procedure which will be so important for the future success of their school in today's deregulated environment.

Contents: Introduction, drawing up the school's mission statement, how to carry out the school audit, planning for the school's development, turning plans into action, taking stock and reporting progress, overview, case study, suggested management exercises, glossary, further reading, index.

A Cambridge graduate, Chris Braund MA PGCE MPhil MEd is a Senior Lecturer in Education Management at Crewe & Alsager College of Higher Education, and Programme Leader for its fulltime MSc course in Education Management. He is actively concerned with training school heads from all over Britain in school management skills, and is a former Regional Committee Member of the British Education Management Association.

Paperback, approx 128 pages, illustrated.

Managing Primary School Staff
Chris Braund

Following the 1988 Education Reform Act, every primary school has become fully responsible for its own professional and non-professional recruitment and staffing, including appointments, staff management and appraisal, terms and conditions of service, discipline, grievances, dismissal and related matters. The freedom of schools to manage their own affairs means important new legal and practical rights and duties for all school managers. Presented in a user-friendly format, *Managing Primary School Staff* meets the urgent need for practical help on a subject of vital importance for the future success of every school.

Contents: Introduction, effective school leadership, the art of deputising, coordinating the curriculum, appointing, promoting and dismissing teachers and other staff, staff support and development, effective staff coummunication, planning for success, case studies, suggested management exercises, glossary, further reading, index.

Paperback, approx 128 pages, illustrated.

The School Library
Elizabeth King MA ALA

Written by a former Chairperson of the School Library Association, this book appraises the role of school libraries in a changing world — a world in which new ideas, new technology and new initiatives (and financial cutbacks) present a special challenge for the professional. 'A stimulating appraisal of the role of the school library in a changing educational world of cutbacks, information technology and educational reform.' *Junior & Middle School Education Journal.*

Paperback, 112 pages, illustrated.

The School Meals Service
Nan Berger OBE FHCIMA

The importance of the school meals service is becoming better recognised today, following greater interest in diet and health, and the advent of privatisation and what it means for standards of service in the educational system. This new book meets the longstanding need for an introduction to—and defence of—the School Meals Service. Expert, readable and forthright, it reviews key health and management issues for everyone having a professional interest in children's welfare, from head teachers and governors to catering managers and educational administrators.

Contents: Foreword, acknowledgements, the beginnings, what the service is and does, the structure of the service, training, nutrition, organising the production of school meals, the stigma of the free school meal, the competition, the problem of midday supervision, the economics of the School Meals Service, the effects of the Education (No. 2) Act 1980, the role of the Government, the future of the School Meals Service, appendices (organisations, statistics, notes on Scotland and Northern Ireland), chronology, bibliography, index.

'Informative, thought-provoking and controversial.' *Lunch Times*. 'Maori-style cooking has not, to my knowledge, been much practised by our own School Meals Service, though no doubt ungrateful children would have their parents believe otherwise. The kind of folklore perception of school dinners is tackled in Nan Berger's School Meals Service. There is much more to the book than this, however, for it is a thorough and well documented history of the meals service, starting with its origins in the last century and moving on to recent traumas of privatisation and closure.' *Times Educational Supplement*. Nan Berger OBE FHCIMA is former Editor of the *National Association of School Meals Organisers Handbook* and *Hospitality* magazine.

Paperback, 144 pages, illustrated.